THE
MYSTERIUM

David Bramwell
& Jo Keeling

THE
MYSTERIUM

Unexplained and extraordinary stories
for a post-Nessie generation

David Bramwell
& Jo Keeling

BREWER'S

First published in Great Britain in 2017 by Brewer's, an imprint of Chambers Publishing Limited.
An Hachette UK company.
Brewer's ® is a registered trademark of Chambers Publishing Limited.
Copyright © Jo Keeling and David Bramwell
The right of Jo Keeling and David Bramwell to be identified as the Authors of the Work has been
asserted by them in accordance with the Copyright, Designs and Patents Act 1988.
Database right Chambers Publishing Limited (makers)
British Library Cataloguing in Publication Data: a catalogue record for this title is available
from the British Library.
Library of Congress Catalog Card Number: on file.
ISBN 9781473663565
eISBN 9781473663572

The publisher has used its best endeavours to ensure that any website addresses referred to in this
book are correct and active at the time of going to press. However, the publisher and the author have
no responsibility for the websites and can make no guarantee that a site will remain live or that the
content will remain relevant, decent or appropriate.
The publisher has made every effort to mark as such all words which it believes to be trademarks. The
publisher should also like to make it clear that the presence of a word in the book, whether marked or
unmarked, in no way affects its legal status as a trademark.
Every reasonable effort has been made by the publisher to trace the copyright holders of material in
this book. Any errors or omissions should be notified in writing to the publisher, who will endeavour to
rectify the situation for any reprints and future editions.

Printed and bound in Great Britain by CPI Group (UK) Ltd., Croydon, CR0 4YY.
Chambers Publishing Limited policy is to use papers that are natural, renewable and recyclable
products and made from wood grown in sustainable forests. The logging and manufacturing processes
are expected to conform to the environmental regulations of the country of origin.
Carmelite House
50 Victoria Embankment
London EC4Y 0DZ
www.chambers.co.uk

Also available
as an ebook

Editor: Jo Keeling
Art director: Tina Smith
Designer: Johnathan Montelongo
Production: Dave Perrett
Research: Guy Lochhead

CHAPTER ONE

strange fruit

CHAPTER TWO

ghosts in the machine

CHAPTER THREE

are we not human?

foreword

Eighty years ago, to the very day that this introduction is being written, American aviator Amelia Earhart disappeared somewhere over the Pacific Ocean. No one knows what happened to her, but boy do we have some awesome theories: she was captured by the Japanese and spent the entire Second World War broadcasting propaganda over the radio under the name 'Tokyo Rose'; she was abducted by aliens; or perhaps, as the book *Amelia Earhart Lives* (1970) insists, she anonymously returned to the US and lived out her life as a suburban housewife named Irene Bolam.

Of course, no one has accepted any of these theories as fact – especially Irene Bolam, who was furious about it – and so the mystery endures. To this exact day in fact – 2 July 2017 – when, over 9,000 miles from where I'm sat typing these words, a pack of four bone-sniffing dogs are wandering around the tiny island of Nikumararo, hunting for her remains.

These highly trained border collies, which can sniff out burial sites that date back as far as 1,500 years up to nine feet underground, are the latest bright idea of an obsessed team who, over the last three decades, have led 12 similar missions attempting to locate the missing pilot.

Why the need for dogs that can smell as far down as a nine feet, you ask? Because this time around they're investigating a new theory: that Earhart survived the crash and lived on Nikumararo as a castaway, but then met her death by giant killer coconut crabs, who ate her, stole her bones and then hid them in their underground burrows. That's an actual theory.

Why are we still fascinated by Amelia Earhart? For some, it's the sheer mystery of it all. For others, it's the need to solve a case. Just like crime writer Patricia Cornwell, who became so convinced of her theory, that Jack the Ripper was the painter Walter Sickert, that she has spent more than $6 million buying up his paintings to prove it (even reportedly shredding two of them in search of clues). Or ex-footballer Gary Lineker, who revealed in January 2017 that he's been quietly trying to work out why every month, for the last 20 years, someone has been sending him a single sheet of used toilet paper in the post.

Even Sir Edmund Hillary, who definitely had more important things to do at the time, revealed that upon reaching the summit of Mount Everest, he couldn't help but look for signs that George Mallory and Andrew Irvine had got there before him. According to Mallory's daughter, her father was carrying a photo of his wife with him, which he was going to leave on the summit. Sadly, Hillary found no photo, nor did he find any other evidence.

So far, none of the above-mentioned mysteries – Earhart, Ripper, Mallory, that weird toilet paper guy – have been solved. Should we give up on them? Never. In 1999, an expedition was launched to search for Mallory and Irvine's camera on Everest. Had they reached the summit, the camera might contain a photo of them doing so. Within two hours, the team stumbled on something completely unexpected: the body of a man on whose shirt was a name tag that read 'G. Leigh Mallory', his body eerily preserved by nature's freezer. On the body, they found Mallory's personal belongings, still in perfect condition some 75 years on – his knife, still in its leather casing; a pair of snow goggles, unbroken; and his brass altimeter. It was an astonishing discovery. The one thing they didn't find though, rather devastatingly, was his camera.

Amelia Earhart and George Mallory are not included as stories in *The Mysterium*. And for good reason – they are far too well documented, and are much better served up as an appetizer ahead of what you are about to read. What David and Jo have so brilliantly done with this tome, is they've forced open a gap in that bookshelf labelled 'mystery' and wedged in something original and different to remind us of all the many new mysteries out there worthy of our eagle-eyed attention. There is more to be marvelled at than just Bigfoot and Roswell.

If you're anything like me, by the time you finish reading this book you will know the rules to a potentially fatal, dimension-shifting elevator game – daring yourself to play it; you will undoubtedly find yourself with ears poised listening out for that unexplainable Earthly 'hum'; you will be sitting with eyes glued to your computer waiting in anticipation for the appearance of the next mysterious Cicada 3301 puzzle; and you'll watch in fascination at the evolution of the terrifying Slenderman as his mythology grows and grows.

So go now and get stuck into the world of *The Mysterium*, soak up all the stories, ponder all the clues, start making your own new connections and – if you can – put those ideas out into the world for others to chew on. Time may pass, landscapes may change, evidence may erode, but as long as there is someone out there who, 80 years down the road, is still willing to say 'What about using bone-sniffing dogs?', these stories are kept alive.

We may never know the answer to any of these strange tales. Perhaps what really matters is that we never stop getting that tingle down our spine when we discover a new enigma or another twist in an enduring mystery – such as the fact that another thing they didn't find on Mallory's body, that day in 1999, was the picture of his wife. DS

Dan Schreiber is a comedian, host of the *No Such Thing As A Fish* podcast, and creator and founding producer of the BBC Radio 4 series *The Museum of Curiosity*.

introduction

'There is a theory which states that if ever anyone discovers exactly what the Universe is for and why it is here, it will instantly disappear and be replaced by something even more bizarre and inexplicable. There is another theory which states that this has already happened.'
Douglas Adams, *The Hitchhiker's Guide to the Galaxy* (1979)

In 2015, Guinness World Record holder, Steve Feltham, hung up his binoculars and headed home. For 24 years, living in a loch-side caravan in Scotland, he had waited for a sighting of the Loch Ness Monster until reaching the inevitable conclusion that it was, in all likelihood, a catfish.

Nowadays, many of us feel nostalgic for a more innocent age when we poured over compendiums of 'the unexplained'. One firm favourite was the Reader's Digest *Mysteries of the Unexplained: How Ordinary Men and Women Have Experienced the Strange, the Uncanny and the Incredible* (1985). Their 'endless search for answers' immersed us in fantastical tales of prophesy and atmospheric oddities, and blurry photos of Nessie, Big Foot and flying saucers. But while a lack of credible proof in our digital age casts doubt over such stories, the universe is as mysterious to us now as it was for our predecessors.

Where we once struggled to understand such phenomena as lightning, eclipses or phases of the moon, now we have to wrestle with the baffling behaviour of subatomic particles or our inability to 'find' 85 per cent of the known universe, known as dark matter. While science remains our greatest means by which to examine the world around us, the very tool essential to interpreting its discoveries remains the greatest mystery of all – consciousness. Can we really understand the universe when we can't understand ourselves?

Where ancient mysteries used to take root and grow organically, passed down through generations through storytelling, now we are globally connected. Far from debunking the unknown, the internet has become a breeding ground for new enigmas. Technology gives mystery renewed strength; stories escalate quickly. One of the most disturbing examples of this is Slenderman (Chapter Two). Born of a 2009 competition to 'create paranormal images', Slenderman's mythology manifested within the space of ten days. Five years later, a ghoul created entirely on the internet starting claiming real-life victims. Elsewhere in Chapter Two, we explore the internet's most enigmatic puzzle – Cicada 3301, the mysterious creator of Bitcoin and the myths surrounding the Dark Net.

If we see films as a cultural expression of our inner anxieties, it's clear that abnormal weather and mysterious atmospheric phenomena tap into a primal fear. Perhaps it's down to the very real threat of climate change or the fact that so much of what happens in our skies and oceans is still unexplained. In Chapter Five, we investigate aurora borealis that can blow up pylons and wipe our bank accounts; balls of electricity that appear inside plane cabins and float down the aisles and dark lightning that shoots gamma rays into space so powerful it can blind sensors on satellites and create anti-matter. While we're unable to offer proof of mythical monsters still roaming the Earth, this chapter does include some curious kitties whose talents range from predicting death to leading a long-established political party.

Over the next 240 pages, we've curated 40 truly compelling mysteries, oddities and remarkable tales for the digital age – from the modern-day powers of placebo to *Hikikomori*, which sees a million Japanese youngsters withdrawing from human contact, to the Melanesian cult that worships Prince Philip as a God and scores of detached human feet that wash up on a beach in British Columbia. As with our previous book *The Odditorium: The tricksters, eccentrics, deviants and inventors whose obsessions changed the world* (Hodder & Stoughton, 2016), each chapter concludes with a seekers' directory, which recommends books, podcasts, documentaries and field trips so you can further explore the mysteries contained within *The Mysterium*.

At the very heart of the human condition lies a paradox: deprived of mystery, life loses its meaning. We seek solace from the rational world through art, film, literature, music, comedy, myth and, nightly, through the surreal fantasia of dreams.

In *The Arabian Nights*, the storyteller confides his secret to Sheherazade: 'We need stories more than bread itself. They teach us how to live and why.' Some of the mysteries in this book might prove to be gateways to new stories, enduring myths from which we continue to dig deeper into the true nature of ourselves. Others may eventually be dismissed or explained away. As Douglas Adams wryly observed, one thing we can be certain of is that today's mysteries will, in the future, be replaced by something even more bizarre and inexplicable.

DB & JK

strange fruit

1:01

Paper phantoms

Trap streets and Mountweazels

Lillian Virginia Mountweazel led a short but creative life. Born in Bangs, Ohio, in 1942, she grew up to be a celebrated photographer whose studies of rural American mailboxes, Parisian cemeteries and New York buses were exhibited across many parts of the globe. Tragically, in 1973, while on an assignment for *Combustibles* magazine, she died in an explosion. She was born in Bangs and went out with a bang, an irony that no doubt amused the creators of the 1975 edition of *New Colombia Encyclopaedia* in which she featured. Not because they were heartless monsters who revelled in schadenfreude, but because Lillian Mountweazel didn't really exist; she was a work of fiction, made up by the encyclopaedia's creators. Her surname has since become a catch-all to denote any deliberately invented word, name or place. But why was Lillian invented in the first place?

A long-standing problem for cartographers and makers of dictionaries, thesauruses and encyclopaedias is how to stop some sneaky bugger plagiarizing years of painstaking research and work, then passing it off as their own. The solution: to set a trap. Dictionaries

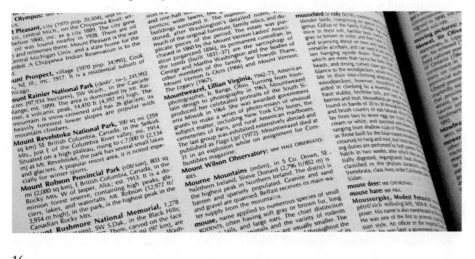

have long been secreting invented words into their tomes to catch out the unwary plagiarists. Should their handiwork turn up in a rival publication, the proof of the pudding is there. Some Mountweazels however, like the word '**esquivalience**' – planted in the *New Oxford Dictionary* in 2001 – have taken on a life of their own. While dictionary.com quietly removed the word from its site after getting caught with its pants down, knowledge of the word spread and there is evidence that esquivalience has been used in several other publications. Esquivalience now straddles a borderland between being a Mountweazel and a real word.

In the world of cartography, equivalent snares to catch unwary thieves are known as 'paper towns' or '**trap streets**'. With some, such as Lye Close or Noereal Road, the clue can be found in the name. The *London A–Z* is known to contain dozens of trap streets. One such lay between Alpha Grove and Casslis Street in the Isle of Dogs. For a while, its real name, Broadway Walk, had been replaced by Bartlett Place, then later corrected once the cat was out of the bag. Online, Google Maps clearly play it safe – the road appears to be nameless.

In 2008, the village of Argleton in West Lancashire appeared on Google, complete with weather reports, a job site and an estate agent advertising houses for sale. Argleton disappeared two years later. While the site was (and still is) just a damp field in the middle of nowhere, it's worth noting that Argleton is an anagram of G Not Real. While Google never admitted to having created it, Argleton was undoubtedly a paper town (albeit of the digital variety) planted as a trap.

Perhaps the most notable cartographic curiosity is the town of Agloe, which would go on to become immortalized in John Green's novel *Paper Towns* (2008). In the book, the protagonist Margo (whose pet dog is called Myra Mountweazel) indulges in what may be an act of esquivalience, when she disappears, leaving oblique clues as to her whereabouts. The trail eventually leads to Agloe.

Agloe was the creation of two men in the 1930s – Otto Lindberg and Ernest Alpens from America's General Drafting Company (AGDC). Commissioned to make a state map of New York, they used the initials of their names to form the name of a paper town – Agloe – which they dropped into a dirt road intersection in the Catskill Mountains. When it appeared a few years later on a map made by Rand McNally, one of their competitors, they threatened to sue. McNally rightly pointed out that they would lose the case: the town was real; there you would find Agloe General Store, at the

Esquivalience (noun): the deliberate avoidance of official responsibility. For example, nipping off to the pub when you're meant to be speaking at your grandmother's funeral.

A trap street features in a 2014 episode of Dr Who, 'Face The Raven'. It is used as a hiding place for aliens using a 'misdirection system' to remain undiscovered. Fans wanting to locate it will have to travel to Cardiff's Westgate Street where the mysterious thin alleyway can be found. Don't expect to find Martians though, alleyways on British high streets tend to serve a very different function for weak-bladdered men, especially on Saturday nights.

Football chants, rumours of a capital city riddled with made-up streets and a town that only ever existed online – fictitious place names continue to tempt cartographers and bewilder road trippers the world over.

Argleton, Lancashire

In 2008, this phantom town (just south of Ormskirk) appeared on Google maps, together with listings for nearby chiropractors and plumbers, despite being nothing more than an empty field. Once spotted, a media frenzy ensued: was it a misspelling of nearby Aughton? A private joke, relating to the British slang term 'argle-bargle', meaning 'to row'? An anagram of 'Not Real G'? Or had the 'Bermuda Triangle of Lancashire' swallowed a whole town? Answers on a postcard to Argleton.

Beatosu and Goblu, Ohio

These two non-existent towns in Fulton and Lucas counties, respectively, were inserted into the 1978–1979 edition of the official Michigan state map. Beatosu ('Beat OSU!') and Goblu ('Go Blue!') sound rather like the cries of University of Michigan football fans against rival Ohio State University. The made-up towns were removed later that year; the original versions now fetch a handsome price.

London trap streets

BBC TV show *Map Man* (2015), recounts a rumour that the *London A-Z* contains 100 trap streets – roughly one per page. One famous example is Bartlett Place, supposedly named after an employee at the Geographer's A-Z Street Atlas company. The name was removed shortly after being exposed on the programme and is now referred to by its real name, Broadway Walk.

crossroads. The store manager, it appears, had spotted Agloe on a map and decided it to be a good place to set up shop. While the store went out of business within a few years – owing to the fact that there were no houses there – it was sufficient proof that Agloe existed. The popularity of the book and film of *Paper Towns* now brings many sightseers to the spot. Even Google Maps acknowledges it, with a red marker for Agloe's (permanently closed) general store.

'Isn't it ironic? Like rain on your wedding day. It's the good advice

you just didn't take', sang Alanis Morissette on her hit 'Ironic', a song that failed to include any actual examples of irony, merely bad luck. But then, ironically, the fact that her song doesn't include any genuine irony is in itself ironic. As is the history of Mountweazel, a made-up word that has now come to define words that are made up.

Nowadays, online quizzes are known to plant fake questions with searchable fake answers on stooge websites in order to trap those trying to cheat. Mountweazels too are growing in abundance in the digital realm as well as in print. So before you think about copying the information in this book and passing it off as your own, it's worth noting that we have planted several Mountweazels of our own. Spot all three of them and write to us with the correct answers and you could win an all-expenses break for two in Bramwellsville, Kentucky. *DB*

The ultimate selfie opportunity. LEFT: Instagrammer Audrey Ong (right) with actor friends Justice Smith (Left) and Jaz Sinclair (centre). Justice and Jaz starred in the film *Paper Towns* RIGHT: Erin Daminato.

The Toynbee Tiles

Urban UFOs (unidentified flat objects)

In the late 1980s, a cryptic message from an unknown creator began to appear in the streets of Philadelphia. 'TOYNBEE IDEA IN MOViE 2001 RESURRECT DEAD ON PLANET JUPITER' was embedded into roads, pavements and even the middle of busy highways. The Toynbee Tiles, or TTT as they soon became known, were linoleum floor panels, into which words had been carved with a knife and filled with different colours. Each tile was secured into the ground using layers of tar paper which, once driven over by a passing car, would effectively glue them in place. Over time, the layer of paper at the top would be worn away by traffic and weather to reveal a Toynbee Tile. It was an ingenious way of getting a message across

Toynbee Tile at 34th and Chestnut Street, Philadelphia, PA.

– whatever that baffling message actually was. Was it a joke, haiku, cryptic code or just meaningless nonsense? Some long-term residents of Philadelphia thought they could remember some strange message about Toynbee and Jupiter coming over their TV set during the news in the early 80s too. What was going on?

A freshly-laid tile. The writing will be revealed after foot and road traffic has trampled away the tar.

Over the next three decades, Toynbee Tiles continued to appear in roads, not just in Philadelphia but across the US from New York, Boston, Baltimore, Kansas and Chicago to Washington. For a while, they even appeared as far as South America, embedded into the streets of Brazil, Argentina and Chile. To date, over 600 Toynbee Tiles have been spotted and photographed, many more lost or destroyed. Few remain in their locations for long before the authorities see fit to remove them. Whether the tiles were the work of one person or a legion, here was an extraordinary act of monomania made all the more amazing by the fact that after 30 years, not a single person had ever reported seeing their creator at work. As the mystery grew, so did a trail of amateur sleuths and obsessives, determined to unravel the puzzle. Let's follow in their footsteps by looking at a few clues.

CLUE #1: THE MESSAGE ITSELF

2001: A Space Odyssey (1968), based on a book by Arthur C. Clarke, is an extraordinary and ambitious film, the meaning of which has drawn endless speculation. Monkeys? Obelisks? Why does Mr Rigsby from Rising Damp turn up? And what about the ending in which astronaut Bowman – part of a team on a trip to Jupiter – appears to enter another dimension where he encounters himself as a giant baby? For TTT fanatics, this scene could easily be interpreted as 'resurrect dead on planet Jupiter'.

As for the name Toynbee, many believe it to be a reference to the English historian, Albert Toynbee. Others connect it with a short story by American author Ray Bradbury, 'The Toynbee Convector', about the future survival of humanity. To add to the confusion, Arnold Toynbee is also the name of a spaceship in another Arthur C. Clarke story, 'Jupiter V'.

CLUE #2: DAVID MAMET

In 1983, David Mamet wrote a short play called *4 A.M.* It focused on a conversation between a radio presenter and a caller who wanted to raise money to publicize his plan to have all dead human molecules reconstituted on Jupiter 'just like in the movie 2001' which, the caller believes, was based on the writings of Albert Toynbee. His bizarre diatribe is eventually cut short by the presenter and the play is over. Mamet has repeatedly insisted that the idea came entirely from his imagination. Had the Toynbee tiler read the play and fixated on this singular idea?

CLUE #3: FOOTNOTES

While the Toynbee Tiles all took the exact same form in early years, some started to appear with their own sidebar of added text – like a footnote. Much of the text seemed to be the disturbed ranting of the kind of person you really wouldn't want at your wedding. Examples include: 'I'm only one man. I caught a fatal disease and they gloated over it' and 'Now the cult of hellion Jews are searching for more than one hell to get more reward. Murder all journalists, I beg you.' One South American tile, however, included a Philadelphia PO Box address. For those on the trail of the Toynbee Tiler, here was a significant clue.

ON THE TRAIL OF THE TOYNBEE TILER

As TTT proliferated through the noughties, a small team of filmmakers and fanatics traced the Philadelphia address back to a reclusive local man. They also discovered that, in a local newspaper archive from 1983, a man calling himself James Morasco had contacted a journalist to discuss the idea of sending the molecules of the deceased to Jupiter for their full resuscitation. Morasco has also popped up on local radio stations and was so committed, he'd even formed a group, The Minority Association, to spread this idea. As journalists were wont to mock or ignore him, Morasco set to work transmitting his idea on shortwave radio, driving around Philadelphia with an aerial attached to his car so his broadcast even cut into people's TVs. From here, he switched to the idea of the tiles. But how did he go undetected for 30 years?

This tiny tile in Philadelphia measures 4" by 2".

While the filmmakers tracked down the likely culprit to an address, his desire for anonymity was respected. They couldn't help, however, overhearing a neighbour talk about the appalling state of Morasco's car. 'The passenger side doesn't even have a floor,' they complained. In a moment of Holmesian deduction, the filmmakers realized that the tiler could drop his works of art from a hole in his moving car onto any road at any time. The tiles would go largely unnoticed until the top tarred layer came away a few days later to reveal the message beneath, by which point the tile would be firmly embedded into the road.

Mystery solved? Not quite. After 30 years, TTTs continue to appear across the US but in new mutant forms, with different messages known as House of Hades. Is a copycat tiler at work? If so, judging

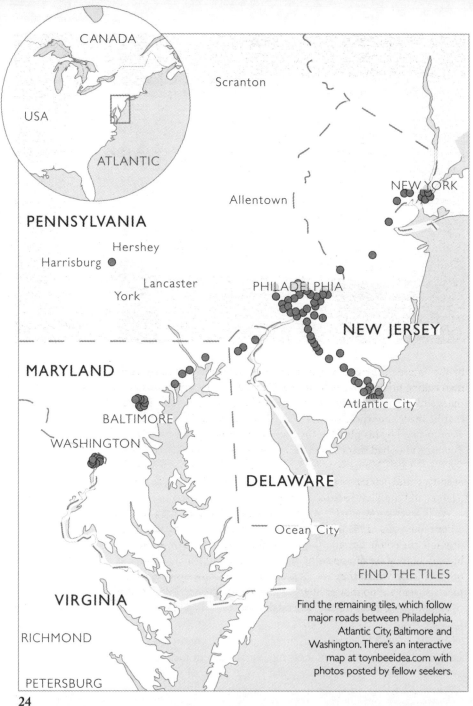

CANADA

USA

ATLANTIC

Scranton

NEW YORK

Allentown

PENNSYLVANIA

Hershey

Harrisburg

Lancaster

York

PHILADELPHIA

NEW JERSEY

MARYLAND

BALTIMORE

WASHINGTON

Atlantic City

DELAWARE

Ocean City

FIND THE TILES

Find the remaining tiles, which follow
major roads between Philadelphia,
Atlantic City, Baltimore and
Washington. There's an interactive
map at toynbeeidea.com with
photos posted by fellow seekers.

VIRGINIA

RICHMOND

PETERSBURG

A 'House of Hades' Toynbee Tile at 19th and Market Street in Philadelphia, showing an evolution of the phenomenon.

by the nature of these new messages, he or she is just as strange as the man calling himself James Morasco. David Mamet – citing this as the weirdest thing that has ever happened to him – doggedly insists that he made the whole story of *4 A.M.* up and that the Toynbee Tiles were inspired by his play. Yet the filmmakers found proof that the Toynbee Tiler had made his baffling phone calls to local radio prior to the existence of Mamet's play. The odds of the tiles and Mamet's play occurring independently of each other are just too improbable, leaving Mamet and the tilers sleuths at a stalemate.

We'll never know what it was that drove the Toynbee Tiler to spend 30 or more years of his life dropping tiles around the Americas to promote the colonization of Jupiter by the dead. And now, slowly but surely, they are disappearing from the streets of Philadelphia and other cities in which they were once planted. As a means of getting a message across – no matter how baffling – the Toynbee Tiles remain to be one of the most ingenious ever devised. *DB*

Panacea's box

Is the Garden of Eden located in Bedford?

From the 1920s to the 1980s, strange adverts were spotted in tabloid newspapers, on billboards and on the sides of British buses. One read: 'England's troubles will increase until the bishops open Joanna Southcott's box.' Another, more explicitly, stated: 'Crime, banditry, distress and perplexity will increase until the bishops open Joanna Southcott's box.'

Those in the know understood that Joanna Southcott's box – the antithesis of Pandora's – contained the secrets of humanity's future happiness; once opened, the problems of the world would dissolve. Two hundred years since its creation (in the early 1800s) however, the box remains unopened, begging the question – why has no one opened the flipping thing?

To unravel the mystery, we need to go back to the 18th and early 19th centuries when Britain was enjoying a fashion for prophesying. Across the land, folk were trying their hand at predicting the future, some more successfully than others. The cream of the crop became known as the Seven Divine Prophets. One of whom, Joanna Southcott, had been a domestic servant in Devon, dabbling in rhyming prophecies, until a friend encouraged her to move to London in 1792 to pursue her calling.

Having correctly predicted the Napoleonic War and two famines, Southcott amassed a large, loyal following and came to believe she was 'the Woman of the Apocalypse', as described in Revelations. Such was her confidence in her own prophecies that Southcott would occasionally send them in sealed containers to different holy men and ask if they could be opened in a few months' time, effectively goading them to give her marks out of ten for accuracy. Had Southcott's followers lived to the 21st century, however, they would have discovered that her claim that the apocalypse would befall us in 2004 proved to be inaccurate (unless you're a music obsessive and believe it was marked by the passing of John Peel).

At the age of 64, Southcott made the surprise announcement that

PICCADILLY CIRCUS – 48 Sheet Poster – June July 1932.

she was carrying the new Messiah, Shiloh, who – the Bible claimed – would be sent from God before Jesus made his return. Southcott's pregnancy became the news story of 1814. On the day she was due to give birth, however, the new messiah failed to materialize. While her most loyal supporters, by now numbering 100,000, believed that Shiloh had bypassed Earth and shot straight to heaven, the 'phantom pregnancy' lost Southcott many devotees. Two months later, she was dead.

Like the other six Divine Prophets, Southcott's name would have faded into obscurity were it not for the legacy of her box. Before her death, Southcott had presented a large wooden box to her followers. Not only did the mysterious locked box contain important prophecies, she informed them, but the act of opening it would herald the return of Christ and a thousand years of peace. The opening of the box, however, came with a caveat – it required the presence of 24 bishops from the Church of England who needed to pray for the box for three days solid, prior to its opening.

Piccadilly Circus, 1932 – a bizarre billboard advert appears urging us to open Joanna Southcott's Box, in order to save the world from crime and perplexity.

27

CRIME
AND
BANDITRY
DISTRESS
AND
PERPLEXITY
WILL INCREASE
UNTIL
THE BISHOPS
OPEN
JOANNA SOUTHCOTT'S
BOX

KENSINGTON, High Street. — 16 Sheet Poster — June, July 1932.

Kensington High Street, 1932.

Bishops, being busy fellows and sceptical of Southcott's claim, were not forthcoming. While Southcott's disciples were only too keen to establish peace on Earth for the whole of humanity, the requisite bishops just would not budge. The box passed down through generations of Southcott's followers and might have ended up as jumble sale fodder were it not for the arrival of Mrs Mabel Barltrop.

MESSAGES FROM GOD AND THE PERFECT BAKED POTATO

Barltrop was born in 1866 and married young to an Anglican priest. By 1906, she was widowed, melancholic and – worse still – living in Bedford. During the horrors of the First World War, Barltrop read about Southcott's box and her legacy as 'the Woman of the Apocalypse', and she began a campaign to have the box opened. It attracted a group of like-minded women who were disillusioned with the conventional patriarchy of Christianity. A small community began to form, creating a 'campus' around Barltrop's house in Albany Road and leading to the establishment of The Panacea Society in 1919.

28

It wasn't long before one of the society's members, Ellen Oliver, had a vision that Barltrop was the eighth (and final) Divine Prophet and a reincarnation of Southcott's phantom child and messiah, Shiloh. While Barltrop was more than receptive to the idea, it was decided that she might not be able to pull off being a male messiah and so Shiloh was renamed Octavia, to fit with **The Panacea Society**'s unique doctrine. The group had developed a 'fourfold' approach to their faith, seeing God as the father, Jesus the son, the Holy Ghost as mother and Octavia as daughter; a more gender-balanced normal family, a bit like the Addams Family.

Barltrop took to her new role as Octavia like a duck to water and was soon receiving direct messages from God every day, promptly at 5.30pm. The messages were a mixture of prophecies and table manners; on one occasion, God gave clear instructions on how best to tackle a baked potato. Male visitors were asked never to wear red or pink bow ties; apologies were due if they were unable to wear a dark suit for evening dinner. God also informed Octavia that her late husband had been a reincarnation of Jesus, which did stretch the credulity of some members of the group, along with the incestuous implications that she'd actually married her brother.

As well as campaigning for the opening of the box, the Panacea Society came to believe that their purpose was to prepare for a visit from God. In their eyes, Bedford was 'the new Jerusalem', and the real Garden of Eden had actually been located in the allotment area of one of their houses.

In accumulating wealth from its followers, The Panacea Society acquired several houses. One included a room in which 24 empty chairs were placed, awaiting the bishops. Another – The Ark – was established for Jesus himself, the group having reasoned that when he returned to Earth, his first stop would naturally be Bedford. As such, they gave The Ark a makeover, agonizing over what colour curtains and carpets Jesus might prefer. On a more practical note, unsure exactly when Christ would show up, they rented out The Ark to bring in extra income. Tenants were housed on the strict understanding that if the Messiah were to show up, the usual four weeks' notice would not apply and they'd have to push off sharpish to make way for His Radiant Being.

While Octavia had predicted her own immortality, she died in 1934. Twenty years later, after much campaigning, The Panacea Society finally came into possession of Joanna Southcott's box and continued its campaign for the bishops' visit, but to no avail. By now the society's

So what was the panacea? Octavia's 'holy breath', which she breathed into small linen squares, was sent to her many followers. Recipients of the panacea (said to cure everything but cancer) would drop the linen square into water and either drink it or bathe in it.

29

Joanna Southcott's box replica, surrounded by 24 empty chairs, is ready and awaiting the bishops' arrival.

seventy-odd members had also begun to await the second coming of Octavia but this proved fruitless too. When its last member died in 2012, a Trust took over the grounds of the Panacea Society and turned two of the houses into museums. A replica of Southcott's box remains in one of the rooms, still surrounded by 24 empty chairs. To this day, no one seems entirely sure if the real box was ever opened or, for that matter, where it is now. The Trust claim that it's stored under lock and key in a secret place, but can the Trust be trusted? It's doubtful we'll ever know. Like all good mysteries, it's probably best kept that way. *DB*

WHAT HAPPENED
TO THE BOX?

3% It's in the custody of a certain Jewett family, based in Yorkshire, who remain tight-lipped about the whole affair.

8% It was lost decades ago and will probably show up one day on *The Antiques Roadshow.*

12% It was given to the British Museum for safekeeping but the museum staff later opened the box, misplaced the contents, and now it's lost forever.

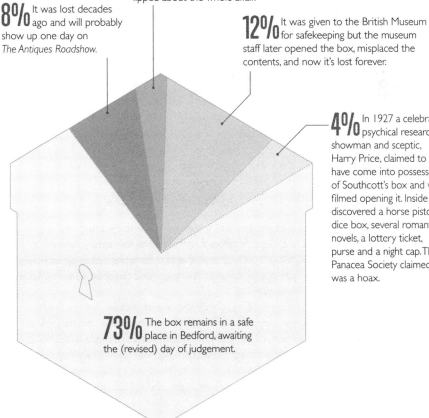

4% In 1927 a celebrated psychical researcher, showman and sceptic, Harry Price, claimed to have come into possession of Southcott's box and was filmed opening it. Inside he discovered a horse pistol, dice box, several romantic novels, a lottery ticket, purse and a night cap. The Panacea Society claimed it was a hoax.

73% The box remains in a safe place in Bedford, awaiting the (revised) day of judgement.

Money burning

Why did The KLF torch a million pounds?

In the early hours of 24 August 1994, the musicians Bill Drummond and Jimmy Cauty entered an abandoned boat house on the Hebridean island of Jura. They were carrying a suitcase full of cash and a lighter. The money was in the form of fresh fifty-pound notes, which they had earned during a hugely successful pop career. Just three years earlier, under the name The KLF, Cauty and Drummond had been the biggest selling singles band in the world. Over the course of an hour, they burned the million pounds. Then they collected the ashes in their suitcase, and returned home.

They were not the first people to burn a million. After President Ford declared the end of the Vietnam War in 1975, and when the North Vietnamese were closing in on Saigon, the evacuating American Embassy didn't know what to do with the million dollars in cash they had in the building. The US Treasury Department told them to burn it. A group of Marines were instructed to carry out this order, and were locked in a room with the money until it was done. It took them eight hours. Drummond and Cauty burned their million in under two hours, which raises the suspicion that the Marines spent the first six hours weeping.

Unlike the Marines, Cauty and Drummond didn't have a reason for burning their money. Or at least, they didn't have an explanation that they could articulate. The pair appeared on talk shows and staged public events during which they expressed the hope that someone could tell them why they had done it. Needless to say, no answer was forthcoming; the public were too angry and appalled to engage with their act on this level. Cauty and Drummond had transgressed the final taboo of the 20th century, and people were not happy about it.

In time, the story of how The KLF burned a million pounds slipped out of the arena of 'crazy music story' and developed into something most accurately described as a modern myth. It was a myth that dealt with every individual's right to reject the norms of capitalist society and to declare that money does not control them. In its wake, the

Money burners view the act as sacrifice and hence a highly spiritual act.

practice of torching cash has slowly spread. It is currently developing into something approaching a movement.

In the world of money burning, intent is everything. Characters such as The Joker in *The Dark Knight* (2008) or Hagbard Celine in the *Illuminatus! Trilogy* (1975) burn money to send a message: they live outside of society's rules, and they cannot be controlled. Money has been burned during political protests, or to prevent others from having it, such as when Serge Gainsbourg burned a 500-franc note on a French chat show in 1984 to protest high taxation. In February 2017, a Cambridge University student was filmed burning a twenty-pound note in front of a homeless man, which led to him being expelled from the Cambridge University Conservative Association. According to the *Daily Mirror*, burning fifty pounds in front of a 'tramp' was part of the initiation ceremony of the Bullingdon Club, the elite Oxford dining club that includes David Cameron and Boris Johnson as former members. The intent behind burning money in this way is simple cruelty. It is only possible by the spiritually bankrupt.

The post-KLF money-burning movement, in contrast, views the action as a modern-day sacrifice and hence a highly spiritual act. Sacrifice occurs in all cultures and is an act deeply wired into our pre-rational minds. Traditionally, it requires a victim, such as a goat, but people burning their own money are both the sacrificer and the victim. This makes it a markedly more potent form of sacrifice and one ethically more defendable. It has more in common with the Norse myth of Odin than traditional animal sacrifice aimed at gaining the favour of the gods. Odin sacrificed himself to himself, by hanging himself from Yggdrasil, the world tree. In return, he received the gift of wisdom.

CREATING A MODERN-DAY RITUAL

Money burning, its modern devotees insist, should not be thought of as an act to produce an intended benefit. It is not an exchange of money for knowledge or an experience of the Divine. It should be an act of selfless giving and, equally, an act of forgiving. It needs to be approached as pure sacrifice, an act of waste that can produce no material benefit. Wasting money by spending it unwisely is very different, for the currency continues to exist and move through the economy as it always does and the money waster at no point steps outside of the everyday world.

The first step in money burning is to select the right amount of cash to set alight. It needs to be just enough to sting. For all but the very rich, this tends to be about twenty quid.

The burning is usually done in private, but it can be done publicly, in groups or on social media. It is recommended that the burner consult his or her own conscience regarding the amount of money that they give to charity beforehand. The burning can then occur with as much ritual as the burner requires. It is sensible to provide a metal bowl to catch the remains of the burning note and to light the currency from a candle rather than fumbling for matches. The burning should then occur in silence, with the burner's attention focused entirely on the flaming currency, from the first lick of fire until the heat burns their fingers and causes them to drop the remains of the note into the bowl.

Those wanting to learn more about money burning should track down *Burning Issue* magazine, which bills itself as the world's first magazine for money burners. *Burning Issue* is edited by Jonathan Harris, who is also the author of *The Money Burner's Manual* (2015). As well as news from the money-burning world and reports from virgin and experienced burners, the magazine contains helpful information, such as how to construct a money bomb. A money bomb consists of a ten pound/dollar note with the words 'Burn Me' written on it, which is placed in a small plastic baggy along with a box

BURNING ISSUE

ISSUE ONE *SPECIAL EDITION* 23RD OCTOBER 2016

NEW IN THE
SPECIAL EDITION

Heathcote Williams
John Lundberg CK Wilde
Mark Wagner + many more

EXCLUSIVE
Dave Lee
CHAOS MAGICIAN
Burn! Blaspheme!
(Dis-)Believe!

CUBE MICROPLEX 22.11.2015

PULL-OUT AND KEEP CENTREFOLD
SPECIAL EDITION
BONUS F23 PIX

AMAZING READER OFFERS !
FREE £$€ NOTE
FOR BURNING INSIDE EVERY ISSUE
PLUS 3 FREE A3 SIZED POSTERS

FIRESIDE TALES FROM VIRGIN BURNERS
"Everyone who had cash took turns"
"Let's burn everything down!"
"Maybe by choosing 23:23 on the 23rd
I had invoked a little bit of chaos"

MAKE A MONEY BOMB !

FULL ASSEMBLY INSTRUCTIONS
FOR YOUR D.I.Y INCENDIARY DEVICE

Mark Carney
Saviour or Antichrist?

John Higgs
C.I.A?

THE WORLD'S FIRST MAGAZINE
EXCLUSIVELY FOR MONEY BURNERS*
*and other destroyers of currency

OUR RECORD OF BURN GUARANTEE: *EVERY SERIAL NUMBER, EVERY NOTE - is yours there?*

containing 23 matches, a folded square of tin foil marked 'Altar', and a cryptic note that reads 'Do what you will – others out there'. The completed money bomb is then left in a public place to be discovered by a random member of the public, who may or may not trigger a blast of new consciousness by detonating it.

But not all is well in the spiritually intended money burning community. As the practice increases in popularity, new polymer plastic banknotes are being introduced (in the UK, at least). These can still be burned, but to do so is unpleasant. It is unlikely that this will put an end to the movement, however, because its practitioners are a determined bunch. Already burners have experimented with destroying digital currencies by copying a Bitcoin wallet onto a memory card, and putting that card into a barbecue.

Whatever the future of money burning holds, it seems unlikely that it will be as powerful and aesthetically perfect as a crisp, brand new twenty-pound note crackling as the aluminium security strip ignites, alone in silent woodland on a clear moonlit night, for no material purpose whatsoever. JH

CONDUCT YOUR OWN MONEY RITUAL

1 Get a fresh, crisp new twenty-pound note from your local ATM.

2 Place that note in a different section of your purse or wallet to where you usually keep your money. Do not spend it.

3 Every few days, remove the note and examine it. Consider to what extent it is just a piece of paper and to what extent it is not just a piece of paper.

4 After keeping the note for a month, remove it from your purse and decide what to do with it. Your options are to spend it, save it, give it away or burn it.

5 Choose the option you consider to be best for your soul and carry it out.

The Anarchist Cookbook

The world's most dangerous book

'This book is not for children or morons.'
William Powell

So concludes the introduction to a book so controversial that, despite
being published almost 50 years ago, there are many still clamouring
for its withdrawal – not least the author himself, William Powell, right
up until his death in 2017.

The book in question is *The Anarchist Cookbook* and there is no
pussyfooting around its intentions. It was wilfully created as a DIY
guide for spreading anarchy, violence and dissent; it is often described
as a 'manual for terrorism'. But could a book with instructions on how
to build booby traps have been deliberately booby-trapped itself?

In the late 1960s, William Powell was a counter-culture dropout,
working as manager in a Greenwich Village bookstore. He was also
required to serve in the Vietnam War and, despite turning up drunk,
high and aggressive at draft interviews – in order to appear unfit for
service – Powell was convinced that the US military was hellbent on
sending him to his death. His response was to quit his job and begin
working on a book that he believed would reveal to the masses the
means by which to win their own freedom. 'Freedom is based on
respect, and respect must be earned by the spilling of blood,' he would
later write in the opening section of *The Anarchist Cookbook*.

Powell's book was published in 1971 and, as its wily publishers
had hoped, caused a huge amount of controversy. Within its pages
are recipes to make LSD, tear gas, nitroglycerine and TNT. It details
combat and guerrilla training, shows how to make a grenade launcher
and Molotov Cocktail, how to booby trap a bridge and ends with tips
on what to do if busted by the cops.

The Anarchist Cookbook outraged everybody, from the law-abiding silent majority – who Powell claimed the book really was for – to the anarchists themselves, who criticized Powell as a sellout, capitalizing on 'the revolution'. During a press conference, one disgruntled anarchist lobbed what looked like an explosive at the author, causing him to run for cover. It turned out to be a stink bomb.

Not everyone was convinced about the book's authenticity either. There were some in the counter-culture who, on learning that Powell's father was a bureaucrat in the UN propaganda ministry, came to believe that he had been put up to the job and deliberately filled the book with dangerous inconsistencies that would lead would-be terrorists or drugs manufacturers to accidentally blow themselves up or blow their minds.

Their paranoia was not unfounded. Powell, barely out of his teens, was no expert on any of the book's material. For research, he claimed to have relied on US military manuals from his local library, drug recipes from the underground press and word of mouth. Could the book's explosive content be trusted? Not according to one reviewer in America's respected *Library Journal*.

> 'There are a number of booby traps for the nitwit who wishes to try them. There are drug making recipes … that may make one very ill … There are also a number of stunts which could backfire on the idiot who tries them.'
> *Library Journal* (15 March, 1971)

By 1976, Powell had disowned his handiwork and converted to Christianity, an act that only served to fuel the fire of the conspiracists. A few years later, his next book couldn't have been more unlikely if he'd written a history of the lawnmower. Granted special interviews with Saudi Arabia's aristocracy, Powell wrote *Saudi Arabia and its Royal Family*, published in 1981. Why did this country's royalty choose to collaborate with such a controversial author as Powell? For some, this was final proof that *The Anarchist Cookbook* was an inside job.

Throughout the ensuing decades, *The Anarchist Cookbook* continued to be published and sold, still containing its myriad errors. In an essay in *Secret and Suppressed* (1993), edited by Jim Keith, the author Esperanze Godot wrote:

> 'The review by the *Library Journal*… exposed these dangerous errors. I wonder why it has gone through 26 printings without these errors being corrected? My theory is that Mr Powell is not an anarchist,

but in reality is spreading disinformation to potential enemies of the government. At the time of original publication, Mr. Powell was an unknown 21-year-old college freshman. Where did he really get access to this "information"?'
Experanze Godot, 'Recipes for Nonsurvival: The Anarchist Cookbook', as quoted in *Secret and Suppressed* (1993)

Powell continued to refute such claims. For much of the next 40 years, he dedicated his time to teaching in Africa and Asia and, in 2010, co-authored *Becoming An Emotionally Intelligent Teacher.*

While information, even video guides, for would-be terrorists are readily available on the internet, *The Anarchist Cookbook* has sold over two million copies worldwide and continues to sell. Perhaps it is Powell's urgent youthful voice that still speaks to disenfranchised outsiders and emotionally volatile teenagers. In some passages, he even manages to be quietly paternal, reminding the reader to respect drugs as 'they are stronger than you are' and 'never to steal from independent shops'.

The Anarchist Cookbook is still linked with myriad acts of terrorism across the globe, including those in Oklahoma City (1995), Boston (2013) and London (2005). In 2016, the book was found in the possession of ISIS terrorists involved in a thwarted plot in the US. A number of American high school massacres – including Arapahoe High School, Columbine and Thurston High – were committed by teenagers in possession of Price's book.

It seems unlikely that Powell colluded with the US government to deliberately fill his book with dangerous inconsistencies. More likely he was, as he often claimed later in life, an angry and alienated young man who came to realize that fighting violence with violence is not the answer. Having signed away the rights to the book before publication, he had no control over its continued reprints. It was, he wryly commented in the documentary *American Anarchist*, 'the most irresponsible publishing event of the century.' DB

SEEKERS' DIRECTORY

Paper phantoms

BOOK *Paper Towns*, John Green (2008), is a coming-of-age drama about a young lad searching for his childhood sweetheart who leaves clues to her whereabouts that lead to the phantom settlement of Agloe. The story was made into a film in 2015.

TV A trap street features in *Dr Who: Face The Raven* (2014) as a hiding place for aliens using a 'misdirection system' to remain undetected. Seek out the mysterious alleyway in question by walking along Westgate Street in Cardiff city centre and looking out for a gap in the wall that allegedly leads to a secret, alien hideout.

FIELD TRIP Take a trip to Agloe, New York, the fake town that briefly became real in the 1950s with a general store, petrol station and two houses. Today, the buildings are abandoned, leaving just a 'welcome to Agloe! Come back soon!' sign. If you do visit, send us a postcard.

The Toynbee Tiles

PLAY The short play *4 A.M.* by David Mamet (1983), focuses on a conversation between a radio host and a caller who's raising money to bring back all dead human molecules to the planet Jupiter via the ideas found in the movie *2001: A Space Odyssey*, which the caller believes is based on the writings of Arnold Toynbee.

FILM *2001: A Space Odyssey* (1968). An excuse to revisit this classic sci-fi, which follows a voyage to Jupiter with the sentient, uptight computer Hal after the discovery of a mysterious black monolith affecting human evolution.

DOCUMENTARY *Resurrect Dead: The Mystery of the Toynbee Tiles* (2011). An independent and award-winning documentary exploring the phenomenon.

FIELD TRIP Visit Philadelphia, especially between Spring Garden Street and Lombard Street, in search of Toynbee Tiles. There's a map, photos and clues at toynbeeidea. com. Best hurry, they won't be there forever.

Panacea's Box

FIELD TRIP Pay a visit to the Panacea Museum and see the box for yourself. Considering that the tea shop actually overlooks the Garden of Eden, the scones are very reasonably priced; panaceatrust.org

DOCUMENTARY *Maidens of the Lost Ark* (2003); A detailed and entertaining exploration of the history of the Panacea Society. Described by *The Guardian* as '*Waiting for Godot* without the jokes'. bit.ly/MysteriumPanacea

Money burning

JOURNAL *The Money Burner's Manual: A Guide to Ritual Sacrifice*, Jonathan Harris (2017), explains why ritual sacrifice is the ultimate moral and spiritual action and why money makes the perfect sacrificial victim.

BOOK *The KLF: Chaos, Magic and the Band who Burned a Million Pounds*, John Higgs (2013). They were the bestselling singles band in the world. They had awards, credibility, commercial success and creative freedom. Then they deleted their records, erased themselves from musical history and burned, their last million pounds in a boathouse on the Isle of Jura. Read the book and find out why.

The Anarchist Cookbook

DOCUMENTARY *American Anarchist* (2016) is a talking head interview with William Powell, author of *The Anarchist Cookbook*.

ghosts in the machine

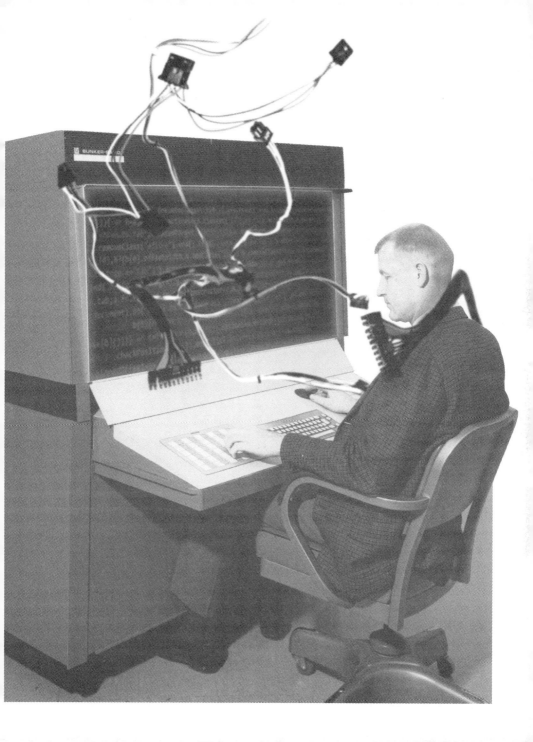

Slenderman

The monster who stepped out of Photoshop and
into our nightmares

At the beginning of June 2014, a singular and grizzly news story
captured the attention of the world press. Two 12-year-old girls from
the Milwaukee suburb of Waukesha, Wisconsin, had attempted to
stab a playmate of the same age to death, inflicting 19 wounds upon
her. According to the reports, they had planned the attack since
February; wanting to lure their friend out to the national park some
distance from their homes, but finally settling for the local woods.

The young girls' expressed intent after their arrest was not simple
murder, but the making of a sacrifice; a bloody call to summon the
attention of a monstrous creature in order to become its Proxies –
obedient, possessed servants. The girls wanted to serve Slenderman.
News organizations hurried to speculate upon this crime's inspiration
– a tall, faceless, suit-clad figure who had first appeared on the internet
as a creation of Photoshopped images, horror stories, YouTube video
series and video games. They sought to understand how something
supposedly unreal could have been the inspiration for such an atrocity.
Within days, two other violent attacks with a Slenderman connection
had occurred. A few days later, it was the fifth anniversary of the
creature's creation. This supposedly imaginary beast had come a long
way in a very short time.

Much of the media coverage focused on Slenderman's backstory, via
a Photoshop competition to 'create paranormal images' on the popular
site somethingawful.com. The posting of Erik Knudsen's initial pair of
images (under the pseudonym of 'Victor Surge') on 10 June 2009 was
the turning point for the competition, and the birth of what became
the first widely known open-source monster. What the majority of
news agencies failed to mention was just how rapidly the Slenderman
mythos had been created and how it left the confines of that website
to become a truly widespread phenomenon. Slenderman as we now
know him manifested in his current form almost entirely within a
mere ten days.

Knudsen's original post consisted of two images of children – one group in a play park, one group fleeing from… something. Both pictures have an indistinct figure in the background – an unnaturally tall man in a suit, possibly faceless and with a suggestion of tentacles for arms. One of the image captions (from the fictional archivist, Surge, who had supposedly kept the photograph) gave the entity that menaced them its name: 'One of two recovered photographs from the Stirling City Library blaze. Notable for being taken the day which 14 children vanished and for what is referred to as 'The Slender Man'.' The other caption read: 'We didn't want to go, we didn't want to kill them, but its persistent silence and outstretched arms horrified and comforted us at the same time…'

HE EXISTS BECAUSE YOU THOUGHT OF HIM

Knudsen's creation dominated the competition thread from that point on. Inspired commenters rapidly added their own pictures, stories, even theories about The Slender Man, whose name was soon shortened to Slenderman. One aspect that was popular from the start was that of providing an alleged historical origin for the creature: he was linked to a variety of mythic figures such as the German

Mediaeval child-stealing 'Der Großmann' or 'Der Ritter' and the Scottish legend of the 'Fear Dubh' or 'Black Man'. Another common theme among the commenters who were not directly adding to the story was that Slenderman was truly unsettling them on a primordial level; some were having nightmares about him. This sense of unease, even dread, was soon folded back into the growing mythology. One post, about a week after the original Knudsen/Surge pictures, read: 'The Slender Man. He exists because you thought of him. Now try and not think of him.'

Symbols have become an important but mysterious aspect of the Slenderman myth. The meaning of the Operator Symbol (RIGHT) is still up for debate. Some claim it simply represents the Slenderman, others claim that it will ward against him.

Like the old saying about hearing the words White Elephant and trying not to imagine a white elephant, many of those who came into contact with Slenderman really couldn't stop thinking about him. The comment thread soon saw even greater expansion of the myth: common aspects and tropes were soon established, such as Slenderman's ability to transcend time and space, and that he cannot be killed.

On 18 June, the first mention was made of what would become the video series that would take Slenderman to a much wider audience in a short space of time. Marble Hornets, a fake 'found footage' horror series, ran for five years on YouTube, further expanding the myth of Slenderman in specific ways. He was shown to have a powerful physical effect on those whose paths he crossed. Symptoms include violent coughing fits, often accompanied with blood, and blackouts; victims losing periods of time from a few hours to three months, during which periods they often perform activities very different from their conscious behaviour – including murder. These possessed victims became known in the mythos as Proxies.

The presence of Slenderman was also shown to have an effect on recording equipment – strange noises creep into the soundtrack when Slenderman (or his Proxies) move into shot. The image itself distorts, flares, and sometimes breaks down into static or apparently random geometric figures. Slenderman's liminal nature gives him an affinity with, and possibly control of, doorways and other passageways. He is seen to appear from rooms previously shown to be empty, or to lure people through doors into places that by all rights should not be accessible through that door.

The widening of Slenderman's fan base was not only reflected in the YouTube series. Hundreds of text-only blogs appeared, the majority telling the personal tales of those who had been affected by Slenderman's baleful influence. Many of these even began to cross over into each other's storylines.

Although Slenderman was not intended as a commercial venture (it remains outside of any claim of copyright or trademark), it was nonetheless soon incorporated into saleable mass media. This is especially true of the popular computer game Slender, in which players attempt to gather information about him while avoiding his attacks. In keeping with the mythos established so early on, players cannot harm Slenderman whatsoever – all they can do is run away. Between the Slender game, the Enderman plug-in for the immensely popular Minecraft game and the release of *Always Watching* (2015), a creator-sanctioned adaptation of the YouTube series Marble Hornets, Slenderman continued to become more of a commercial endeavour.

THE BLURRING OF MYTH AND REALITY
By the start of 2014, the Slenderman phenomenon, though still popular, was seeming to lose ground. Many blogs had closed; others were posting far less frequently. Despite appearances on episodes of TV shows such as *Supernatural* and *Lost Girl*, it seemed that Slenderman was perhaps starting to die from lack of attention.

47

SLENDERMAN

Slenderman fan art ranges from
the macabre to the playful,
such as this Lego rendition.

That is, until the Waukesha incident. This and the later attacks brought tremendous focus onto the Slenderman phenomenon. One in particular brought a new layer of dread. A Hamilton County (Cincinnati) mother told of being attacked by her 13–year-old, Slenderman-obsessed daughter, who wore a white mask as she wielded a kitchen knife at her. 'She was someone else during that attack,' the mother said.

January of 2017 saw the first transmission of an HBO documentary on the Waukesha attack, *Beware The Slenderman*. Although featuring extensive interviews with the assailant's parents and dramatic interrogation and court footage, its examination of the origins of Slenderman was both superficial and factually inaccurate – ironic, in that the mythos has always blurred fact and fancy.

One possible explanation for the rise of Slenderman and its continual crossing between reality and myth can be found in the concept of 'ostension'. In anthropology, ostension is the phenomenon in which real-life events are shaped and influenced by folklore – examples include the fact that the urban legend of poisoned or booby-trapped Halloween candy predates the first known occurrence of such by some ten years. Slenderman – originally a composite of many urban legends, stories and older myths – has now come full circle, becoming the inspiration for real-life actions, which in turn further strengthen that myth.

Slenderman's rise also serves to illustrate that the line between fact and myth which he crosses, even represents, had been blurring for some time. In a world where the Guy Fawkes mask from Alan Moore's *V For Vendetta* is the international symbol for organized disobedience, where democracy protesters in Thailand lift three fingers in the people's solidarity salute from *The Hunger Games* and Jedi Knights have the same civil liberties as any other believer... the distinction between an orthodox religion and a hyper-real belief is looking more like one of degree, not kind.

In another five years, Slenderman may simply be just another imaginary-but-venerated deity among many. How we deal with that – whether these new gods inspire us to creativity or to remorseless violence – will be a reflection of our nature far more than of theirs.

We have to remember too that, whatever else Slenderman may be, he is a creation, a story, a trick of the mind. If he starts troubling you after reading this, take heed. As modern Holy Fool, Pee-Wee Herman once said: 'Your mind plays tricks on you? You play tricks back!' *CV*

John Titor

A benevolent time-travelling Donald Trump?

Cast your mind far, far back to the summer of 2001 if you can. The build-up to our brave new millennium had lasted years, the apocalyptic threat of the Millennium Bug freaked us out and we all confidently expected jet packs to be sold in Asda before too long.

It was into this uncertain mix of doubt and hope that the internet phenomenon of John Titor was born, a mystery never conclusively resolved to this day. There was no fanfare to his arrival; it all took place on humble bulletin boards. Members of an online 'anomalies' community had been pondering the possibilities of time travel, when suddenly a new voice piped up – with an extraordinary claim.

'Greetings,' he said. 'I am a time traveler from the year 2036. I am on my way home after getting an IBM 5100 computer system from the year 1975. My "time" machine is a stationary mass, temporal displacement unit manufactured by General Electric. The unit is powered by two, top-spin, dual-positive singularities that produce a standard, off-set Tipler sinusoid. I will be happy to post pictures of the unit.'

Titor dutifully shared some images of his time machine – a mixture of photos, scanned documents and diagrams. The exploded technical drawings were as professional looking as anything you might find in a washing machine manual. The photos showed a 'device' built into a vehicle with a particularly intriguing one of a laser beam apparently bending in the craft's gravity field.

Never one to hide his light under a bushel, Titor also shared pictures of his flashy military insignia, explaining that his mission was a Government one: he had been sent back in time to acquire a 1970s computer capable of translating a range of languages – useful in a future where digital resources are rare. And just before you get too excited: while the machine's debugging potential was not well-known in the year 2000, it certainly wasn't classified information, either. Titor hung around for three months on these forums and answered a lot of questions about the years to come. He then returned to his future as mysteriously as he had come, and was never seen again.

Like all the best legends, John Titor did not beg us to believe him or to get too bogged down the details of his story, but rather to consider what his words meant, on a deeper level. 'The most I could hope for is that you recognize the possibility of time travel as a reality,' he advises. 'You are able to change your worldline for better or worse just as I am.' This is just as well, as citizens in Titor's 2036 had had a run of bad luck, to say the least.

In his blog posts, Titor described a country devastated by mad cow disease and civil war, where skirmishes between citizens and the military were common. That would be bad enough, but the entire planet was also in recovery from the Third World War, which kicked off in 2015. Every major city in the US was destroyed by Russian nukes, rendering urban areas uninhabitable and killing three billion people. No fewer than five presidents now ruled the country (none of them were orange either), and survivors banded together in back-to-basics enclaves where they worked the fields for food. People lived up trees, rode horses, danced around bonfires, whittled (yes, things had got that bad), and ate beans out of the tin while singing 'Kum Ba Yah'. Like the Wild West, but with internet and time travel.

Titor's colourful future predictions have been unpicked over the years, with many finding current events resonating with his cryptic words. Looking at the US today, however, it's hard not to notice its lack of nuclear devastation. For now, at least.

A TIME-TRAVELLING PRESIDENT?

If you're feeling the doubt creeping in at this point, you're not alone. But there is an argument that might yet convince you. Even as he chats in the forums, Titor claims to notice small details diverging from his timeline's history: 'News events that happen at different times, football games won by other teams, things like that.' So is it possible that Titor was a visitor from another time, and his mere presence in 2001 forever altered the course of history? Or, perhaps, we have been on a slightly different timeline to his all along, and like strands of a fibre-optic cable emerging from the same bundle, it's possible to jump between them.

More recently, even more brazen theories have cropped up. For some online conspiracists, the emphasis on the Russians and the US presidency, along with Titor's slightly rude and abrupt manner, can mean only one thing. That's right: John Titor is Donald Trump. OK bear with this one – the facts are just as weird as the speculation.

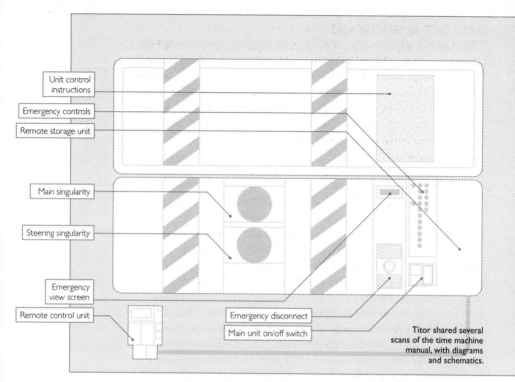

Unit control instructions

Emergency controls

Remote storage unit

Main singularity

Steering singularity

Emergency view screen

Remote control unit

Emergency disconnect

Main unit on/off switch

Titor shared several scans of the time machine manual, with diagrams and schematics.

Implausibly enough, Donald Trump is the nephew of John George Trump, a well-known MIT professor who was invited by the National Defence Research Committee to review Nikola Tesla's work after the latter's death, in 1943. Trump Sr didn't seem to think much of Tesla's research, though, which his official report dismissed for its 'speculative, philosophical, and somewhat promotional character'.

But what if that was all a cunning smokescreen, and John George Trump had, in fact, found the plans for something much more interesting among the physicist's notes? What if there were a few sketches tucked in between Tesla's scribbles on 'wireless electricity' and 'the induction motor' that could, in theory at least, defeat the direction of time itself?

Before John's death in 1985, he spent a lot of time with his nephew and the pair became close. Donald often spoke of his scientist uncle in interviews, relaying in particular his warnings about the rise of nuclear weapons. **Is it so crazy to wonder whether, in addition to these abstract warnings, John left his nephew the means to create a time machine from Tesla's blueprints?**

Erm, yes.

TALE OF THE 88 STOOGES

The theory really writes itself from there. Like a benevolent Biff from *Back to the Future*, Donald Trump used his time machine car to amass enough wealth to enter the electoral race. Only from this position of power could he hope to intercept the terrible chain of events that he had witnessed unfold from the other end, avert the course of history and save us all from nuclear disaster. Unlikely as it sounds, **could Trump actually have travelled from the future to save us all from self-destruction?**

Erm, no.

While a visitor from another time is an extremely appealing idea, scarcely less tantalizing is the mystery of who might concoct a fiction on this scale, and for what reason? After all, 'if it is a hoax,' as one person wrote on a Titor site, 'it's a very elaborate one'.

The question of who might have conceived the hoax, at least, now has a persuasive answer. In September 2003, a not-for-profit organization called The John Titor Foundation was set up, with a rented PO Box in Kissimmee, Florida as its only address. An IP address associated with Titor's posts also geolocates to Kissimmee, and one can't help but notice the time traveller himself talks about growing up in Florida (albeit in the dystopian future). In 2003, the foundation self-published a book, *John Titor, A Time Traveler's Tale* – out of print but reputedly little more than a bound copy of the message board posts. Could all of this have been about promoting a book?

In 2009, the Hoaxhunter website analysed the names of the individuals who had been engaging Titor online, suggesting they were made up by the hoaxers, and pointing out that, 'when you're choosing the questions to ask yourself, it's a bit easier to answer them'. Rather than continuing the conversation about this extraordinary stranger, many of the 88 individuals disappeared from the internet when Titor did. In a delightful twist, Hoaxhunter speculates that the number of stooges is a wink to the *Back to the Future* car's famous time-travelling speed: '88 miles per hour'.

Let's hope that whoever was behind Titor never breaks their silence. Enthusiastic analysis of the legend continues online to this day, and not just because we want time travel to be real or to figure out who he really was. Titor is compelling because it's really a nostalgic story about the past – the recent internet past – a time where creativity and silliness had more space to flourish, in an altogether quieter web. ⑂

Who is Satoshi Nakamoto?

The inventor of the Bitcoin has a lot to answer for – whoever they are

Bankers don't get much love these days. They've probably never had much of a great rep, but since the 2008 financial crisis, the faceless 'banker' has been something of a pantomime villain in the Western world, a symbol of rising inequality (and for good reason, many would argue). But it's this anger at financial institutions combined with the ingenuity of engineers and the counter-culture of the internet that has spawned a whole new currency: Bitcoin.

In essence, Bitcoin works from a fundamental concept in economics and trade that many of us forget: money isn't real. Paper and coins are merely a vehicle by which we trade; they have no inherent value. Similarly, Bitcoin is a virtual currency that can be used to trade in goods and services, except that it is decentralized; it is not constrained by the traditional powers-that-be.

At first Bitcoin gained traction with the Deep Web's black markets, but has now found its way into the mainstream; WordPress started accepting the currency in 2012, followed by OKCupid, Expedia and Microsoft. You can even use it to buy a beer and a burger in central London. However, its use is far from widespread and the lasting impacts of this phenomenon are still evolving, with hundreds of engineers and venture capitalists still investing in its technology despite its volatile nature as a currency based in essentially nothing. But how did it come into being?

THE NAKAMOTO MYSTERY

One night in 2008, a person (or persons) – identified only as Satoshi Nakamoto – used an untraceable email address to publish their new currency idea on a well-known cryptography blog. The paper proposed a new kind of electronic payment system, free from the instabilities of monetary policy making, politics and the predations of bankers. Rather than credit card companies and banks recording your financial transactions in their central ledgers, vouching for you then taking a fee, all of the users would record all of the transactions at the same time on a massive accessible global ledger, called the **Blockchain**. This would create a decentralized network of trade, external from governing bodies other than the users themselves. Free from such constraints, the new currency – Bitcoin – could then be used as a way to trade online.

Between 2009 and 2010, Nakamoto penned hundreds more posts and messages about their innovative software and currency, often inviting developers to improve the code. But then in April 2011, the user posted their final note, stating that they had 'moved on to other things'. They were never (officially) heard of again. This is where the mystery of Bitcoin begins.

WHY IS IT SO IMPORTANT TO KNOW WHO NAKAMOTO IS?

Well, other than old-fashioned curiosity, there are two key reasons why the identity of Nakamoto is so pressing. Whoever they are, they hold an incredible number of Bitcoins, which if unloaded quickly enough and transformed into another currency, or put back into the Bitcoin circulation, could depress the **currency's value** and throw its current economic trajectory to the wind. It would also make Nakamoto one fairly rich computer mastermind.

There has also been an ongoing discussion between developers surrounding increasing block sizes to stop transaction complications and outages (cyberattacks on exchange networks). However, this could serve to concentrate the ability to mine the currency into the hands of the few that could afford to own enough computers with the processing power necessary to mine such blocks. Ultimately, Nakamoto would have the final say on this matter. As it stands, there are few clues left for Nakamoto's followers to go on. We take a look at the most likely candidates over the page.

BITCOIN TODAY

With Nakamoto still 'at large', speculation about the future of Bitcoin is rife. Many believe it's not actually destined to become a globally dominant, mainstream currency. Instead, its key advocates and investors foresee a variety of more intricate implications arising from the technology and architectural design of Bitcoin. Nakamoto's brainchild is now heralded as the possible future of 'micro-payments' (such as in-app purchase on smartphones); a tool to strengthen the

Bitcoin is organized by a network of computers called 'Miners' that anyone can be a part of. When you download Bitcoin software, you are given a digital wallet with a unique identity. When you acquire a Bitcoin, this transaction is broadcast to the Miners. The digital wallets of each party involved sign the broadcast with their unique signature, allowing the Mining computers to validate the transaction and follow each Bitcoin throughout its life.

At the time of publishing, one Bitcoin was worth £1920.04 (xe.com).

1. Craig Wright

In 2016, this Australian entrepreneur and computer science expert revealed himself to be the real Satoshi Nakamoto. However, his claim to the bit-throne is dubious. The cryptocurrency community debunked him because of his inability to validate his identity with 'digital keys' (a kind of digital signature), and reports indicate that he had hired a PR company to fake the whole ordeal because he was struggling with financial problems and a tax investigation. To make matters more suspect, many of Wright's social media accounts and company websites vanished shortly before his announcement. That's not to say this isn't just a very elaborate double bluff.

2. Dorian Prentice Satoshi Nakamoto

A reporter for *Newsweek* pegged a 64-year-old Japanese ex-classified military engineer living in Los Angeles as the inventor in 2014. Unfortunately, Dorian Prentice Satoshi Nakamoto (it's got to be him, right?) flatly denied the allegations. There's a wonderful film on YouTube in which the Californian resident argues that he's not the inventor while being plied with tray after tray of sushi. Following the press, an old account (known to be used by the real Nakamoto) came back online with the message: 'I am not Dorian Nakamoto'.

3. Michael Clear

Analysing lines from the preternatural coder's writings and secret messages hidden in the code, many suggest that Nakamoto is British, or at least educated in the UK. Working off this assumption, sources have pointed to the illusive Michael Clear. At the tender age of 10, Clear was already programming computers with a variety of different coding languages. He graduated in cryptography from Trinity College, Dublin, and was named the top computer-science undergraduate in 2008. By 2009, he was hired by Allied Irish Banks and had co-authored a paper on peer-to-peer technology. Joshua Davis at the *New Yorker* tracked him down in 2011, and Clear casually introduced himself with the words: 'I like to keep a low profile, I'm curious to know how you found me.' Clear has denied his involvement in bitcoin.

4. Hal Finney

Finney was a graduate of the California Institute of Technology and was known for a number of things in cyberspace. He was a key developer in the groundbreaking encryption software PGP, a well-known figure in the 'Cypherpunks' (an early 90s group advocating airtight encryption for individuals) and, most notably, he is credited with receiving the very first bitcoin transaction from Nakamoto. He also denied being the creator of bitcoin, but we may never know for sure as his body is now cryogenically frozen after losing his fight with a neurological disease in 2014. Finney's former address was only a few blocks away from the family home of Dorian Nakamoto.

5. Gavin Andresen

As one of bitcoin's most senior developers, Andresen has been a leader of the movement since 2011. He is a primary force in its continuation through entities such as bitcoin XT and has also openly advocated that Craig Wright (our first suspect) was the real Satoshi Nakamoto. One might consider this a clever ruse, however, as a result of his support for Wright, his position at bitcoin's HQ has now become much more 'ceremonial'. An article from *The Guardian* ('Bitcoin project blocks out Gavin Andresen over Satoshi Nakamoto claims', 2016) states that, as of 2016, Andresen was said to have had his abilities to change the main bitcoin code 'revoked'. Or is that what he wants us to think?

6. Nick Szabo

Our final, and arguably most interesting, candidate for the role of Nakamoto is a reclusive American/Hungarian man whose whereabouts are still an enigma (a mystery within a mystery!). Nick Szabo is a computer scientist, legal scholar and cryptographer. He was the inventor of bitcoin's predecessor bit-gold and his work with many high-profile security firms today remains very secretive. Of course, Szabo has denied his involvement with bitcoin, kindly stating on Twitter 'Not Satoshi, but thank you'.

Bitcoins are widely accepted in the real world, from pubs and pizza chains to an East London man with a van

internet's points of failure; and a vehicle to easily transport money internationally. It might also foresee a new financial phenomena known as 'programmatic finance', the ability for businesses to 'own and run themselves' independently.

Perhaps more importantly, another thing Bitcoin has done since its inception is to call attention to the mysterious nature of money. Through the paradigm of 'digital gold', given value by the 'Miners', we're able to look at how trade and money influence our social world from a whole new angle.

Nakamoto's invention presents a departure from the norm; it is a window into the concept of trade and the supposedly impenetrable beast many refer to as 'the market'. If something 'digital', without substance, can disrupt and find its place within the current economic system – and continue to exist, largely through belief – then we can see that this thing we call 'the market' is actually very much at the whim of real people. From a libertarian point of view, it is something that has been taken out of the hands of the many and put into the hands of the few. In effect, Nakamoto acts as figurehead for engaging with larger governing bodies – those bankers again – that we can't face or question on our own. Perhaps searching for Nakamoto is important because it gives us hope that we, the average human, can change the system.

The identity of Nakamoto reflects the nature of Bitcoin itself – a decentralized entity that is game changing, cryptic and flawed. The unfolding of its story shows us that human's endeavours are not perfect. But Nakamoto is a great example of how human ingenuity can open the possibilities for great paradigm shifts. Might we have a future in which bankers find themselves sat at their desks, twiddling their thumbs and wishing someone, anyone, would send them an email asking if they could borrow a fiver? But then, after all their sterling work these past few years, aren't our poor, beleaguered bankers due a nice long bank holiday? MI

The Deep Web

What lies beneath?

'We need to go dark.'
Alex Winter, actor and director *Deep Web: The Untold Story of Bitcoin and the Silk Road* (2015)

Remember the final terrifying scene in *Paranormal Activity*? The Dark Net is even scarier. All the ghouls and spectres of the internet can be found there, drifting around in its seedy underbelly. It is a portal to a world of untold horrors where hardened criminals and fraudsters lurk. It is a black market of firearms and drugs; home to extreme pornography and recipes for cooking human flesh. In its shadowy hinterland, professional hitmen can be found and – for a reasonable fee – rent-a-hackers may be hired to download illicit images to your nemesis' laptop and then inform the police.

If 95 per cent of all internet activity takes place on the Dark Net – as we are led to believe – the human psyche really is as depraved as our tabloid newspapers would have us believe. But before we indulge in too much righteous indignation and scandal, let's take stock. While some of the above information is true, much of it is exaggerated and sensationalized. To demonize the Dark Net because it harbours criminal activity is to miss the point entirely. It'd be like judging the whole of Star Wars on Jar Jar Binks.

THE DEEP WEB
As there is so much confusion around the Dark Net, we'll start by clearing one thing up: the Dark Net and the Deep Web are not the same. When we're told that search engines only reveal 5 per cent of all web activity, this doesn't mean the other 95 per cent – the Deep Web – is brimming with hitmen, dealers and cannibals. Most activity on the Deep Web is simply unindexed content that search engines cannot find: Google docs and Dropbox contents, databases, emails, journals, medical records, academic information and government resources.
The Dark Net (or Dark Web) is a very small part of the Deep

Web that has been intentionally hidden from search engines. It is decentralized and accessed through a Tor browser – The Onion Router – so named because its users are hidden behind umpteen layers of encrypted codes (like the layers of an onion). In the Dark Net, rather than going straight to a website via its URL, Tor is effectively like asking a friend of a friend of a friend (etc.) to supply you with the information. Except they'll never really be your friends – you all remain anonymous to each other.

The Dark Net has been quietly operating for many years, but really came to public attention after news broke about one of its websites, Silk Road, which sold illegal drugs, firearms and nefarious services in a format similar to eBay. Here, anonymity was guaranteed – all sales were done using the cryptocurrency Bitcoin. Because of stiff competition on Silk Road, dealers needed to earn a good reputation. Compared to illegal street drugs – whose impurities are the main cause of all drug casualties – the quality of drugs on Silk Road were far superior. Why loiter in an alleyway waiting for a shady dealer when you could place your orders at home and be far less likely to buy a product laced with household cleaning products? For the stoner with a conscience, some dealers on Silk Road even claimed their goods to be locally sourced, organic and fair trade. Top quality narcotics, combined with expedient and polite transactions, led Silk Road to receive unparalleled customer satisfaction – 98 per cent of all transactions were five stars, far higher than anything Amazon or eBay could guarantee.

After two years' close surveillance by the FBI, human error led to Silk Road being closed down. Its founder, Ross Ulbricht, was given two life sentences which, the judge claimed, was to give 'a clear warning to others'. Within a few weeks, several similar sites had already taken its place. One thing we can be sure of, while recreational drugs remain prohibited, the law of supply and demand means that such exhaustive and expensive cat and mouse games will never end.

But even to focus on this is to miss the wider picture. According to Jamie Bartlett, author of *Dark Net* (2014), the most widespread illegal activity on the Dark Net isn't making heroin-fuelled kitten torture-porn but simply the sale and purchase of marijuana, a drug that, increasingly, is being decriminalized across parts of America and Europe.

For the unwary traveller, the Dark Net is best approached with caution. There are, however, plenty of websites and YouTube guides offering practical advice for newbies. It is useful, perhaps, to think of

BELOW THE
SURFACE

Surface web
Cats, porn, eBay, Amazon,
porn, Kim Kardashian's
bottom, dictionaries, cats,
clickbait, calculators, porn,
cats, translation engines,
Justin Bieber, porn, cats.

Deep Web
Databases, online libraries,
academic resources,
registration-required web
forums, email accounts,
bank accounts, web
archives, private websites.

The Dark Net
Anonymity, the freedom
to publish and exchange
information without
recrimination, whistle-
blowing, drug sales, fake
hitmen, rent-a-hackers,
90s throwback aesthetic.

The Marianas Web
Secrets of Atlantis, Bavarian Illuminati,
unicorns, weird-looking fish with
Donald Trump's hands, Lord Lucan,
that really expensive jumper you
lost, the identity of Chuck Tingle,
pink M&Ms, Marianas Wombles (well,
someone's got to keep the place tidy
haven't they?)

entering the Dark Net as a trip to Amsterdam. While some may seek cheap thrills, others may prefer to enjoy a quiet area of the city, free from chain stores and advertisements, hang out in a few cafes and chat with some like-minded folk in a tolerant atmosphere (the Dutch are, after all, a pretty chilled out nation). And this is actually what the majority of users enter the Dark Net to do – speak freely.

Set up by the US Navy Intelligence in 1972 to allow a voice for activists supported by the American government, the Dark Net remains a safe haven for those seeking anonymity. It offers secure communication for whistleblowers, dissidents, journalists and those living under oppressive regimes to speak their minds. It is a safe place for news drops, Wikileaks and file sharing. It played a vital role in movements like the Arab Spring Uprisings and undoubtedly will again.

DEEPER STILL

Further down still, far beneath the Deep Web, lies **the Marianas Web**, the internet's equivalent of Atlantis. Legend decrees that the Marianas Web is so mysterious, vast and secret that the only access is via a network of quantum computers, which is a little bit tricky as they don't really exist yet. Minor technical details and reality aside, once entered – like a less 'doomy' version of Indiana Jones' Temple of Doom – it is said to unveil the great secrets that have eluded us for millennia. This is said to be the home of the Illuminati and the Holy Grail (the cup, not the film), it is where all state secrets are hidden and, curiously the true location of Atlantis can be found. Most paradoxical of all, the only place to discover the secret portal to the Marianas Web is ... the Marianas Web.

We live in an age where our hopes of an egalitarian internet have long since been dashed. It is now controlled by a handful of global corporations and billionaires and is saturated with advertising, pop-ups, clickbait and algorithms logging our every move and word. We are under surveillance from governments and multi-nationals, harbouring a growing uncertainty as to who has rights and access to our emails, accounts and photos, especially after we die. With the utopian promise of the internet dead and gone, the Dark Net may be our best hope of reclaiming our anonymity and freedom of speech, in a virtual world mercifully free of the words: 'what she did next will astound you'. DB

If the Marianas Web really is a repository of all the world's great secrets, our editor lives in hope that one day she will finally discover the identity of the flatmate who put her bedsheets in the freezer in the summer of 2008.

Cicada 3301

The internet's most enigmatic puzzle

In 2012, a puzzle appeared on the internet that was so fiendish to crack it required a working knowledge of cryptography, steganography, computer coding, obscure works of fiction, ancient Mayan numerals and advanced music theory. It contained the kind of clues that perplex even the most ardent cryptic crossword-solvers and required participants to find physical clues in the real world as well as areas of the internet that look like the seedier areas of downtown Mars in *Total Recall*.

The puzzle, named Cicada 3301, emerged when users surfing the anonymous channel 4chan found a white-on-black image that read:

'Hello. We are looking for highly intelligent individuals.
To find them, we have devised a test. There is a message hidden in the image. Find it, and it will lead you on the road to finding us. We look forward to meeting the few who will make it all the way through.
Good luck.'

While some assumed it was just a prank, others found their interest piqued and began to unearth more levels to the puzzle. The first message led participants through a variety of complicated stages, which required them to use knowledge of ancient Mayan numerals to decode a piece of text; detect steganography (data hidden within data) to reveal hidden riddles; ring a Texan phone number outside of the web for a recorded message; and to co-operate internationally with other users across the world.

The puzzles appeared on 4 January 2012 and then, again, on the same date in 2013 and 2014. Whoever set them was highly intelligent and not working alone. They also had a penchant for prime numbers, music and interesting texts. They knew their way around chat forums, computer programming and the Dark Net.

Only a very few people were able to solve the Cicada mystery in the first year. One who nearly made it was Joell Eriksson, a crypto-security researcher from Sweden who navigated his way through the multi-layer mystery until he reached a countdown website telling him to come back on an allotted day. When he returned, he was presented with a list of worldwide GPS coordinates where flyers printed with QR-codes were taped to posts. The QR scans led to clues within the William Gibson *Agrippa* poem – and from there to an address on the Dark Net. By the time he completed that puzzle, a message had been posted to the effect that Cicada 3301 were 'disappointed' with the amount of group sharing some people were doing to solve the clues. How they knew remains unknown, but the drawbridge was pulled up before Eriksson could get in.

Others got further. In 2015, Marcus Wanner, a previous Cicada 3301 alumnus, talked to *Rolling Stone* magazine. He had made it through and had received a message:

> '… we are an international group. We have no name. We have no symbol. We have no membership rosters. We do not have a public website and we do not advertise ourselves… We are drawn by our common beliefs, that tyranny and oppression of any kind must end, that censorship is wrong and that privacy is an inalienable right.'

They went on to say that they were not a hacker group, nor did they engage in or condone illegal activities. They likened themselves to a thinktank with a primary focus on 'researching and developing techniques to aid the ideas we advocate: liberty, privacy, security'.

New recruits were given a username and password and invited to join a forum where they were introduced to other successful clue-solvers and to a few 3301 mentors. They were grouped into teams to work on specific projects. Wanner's project was called CAKE (Cicada Anonymous Key Escrow System), in which group members were to write a programme that would automatically publish certain sensitive data should the originator die or become incarcerated.

While Wanner and a few others tell us snippets about their association with the group, we still don't know many details and, of course, the beauty of vague and uncorroborated information is that it leaves plenty of room for other speculation. Some theories suggest a government agency (CIA, NSA, MI6?) are involved, others think it is some sort of global banking network or political think tank looking for the best analytical thinkers. There are those that believe Cicada is a secret society, a cult or some amoral group of anarchist hackers.

Among the stranger ideas is the notion of artificial intelligence that has outsmarted its creators; alternatively, much as in the Matrix series, this is a test to see if we're ready to accept that we are each just a string of data on a huge computer; and finally, the theory that aliens are using Cicada as an assessment to see if the human race is prepared to be benignly forced into 'the next stage' of our evolution.

Whatever the answer, we know that they have a bizarre and eclectic interest in ancient and underground literature. *Agrippa*, for example, is **a poem by William Gibson** used in the first Cicada mystery. There are very few hard copies in existence and it was always meant to represent the transitory nature of stories.

Other works included those by William Blake, and famed occultist Aleister Crowley's *Liber Al vel Legis* (or *The Book of the Law*, said to have been told to him through a mysterious disembodied voice) and texts derived from such diverse sources as Jung, Nietzsche, Rasputin, Sartre and Zen Buddhism. No surprise, then, that the Cicada 3301's final conundrum should come in the shape of a book.

The Liber Primus is the last incomplete part of the Cicada puzzle. Originally a section of the 2014 challenge, a message was posted with a link to a Tor page that led to a series of jpeg images. Each image appeared to be a page of runic text and it soon became clear that these pages made up a full book: The Liber Primus (which translates as 'The First Book of Letters'). This was originally considered to be simply a vessel within which a small part of the 2014 puzzle was hidden; however, when there were no new posts from Cicada in 2015 (except for two messages disputing the group's involvement in two acts of internet activism) people began to suspect it represented more. Then, in 2016, a new message was posted:

Hello.
The path lies empty; epiphany seeks the devoted.
Liber Primus is the way. Its words are the map, their
meaning is the road, and their numbers are the direction.
Seek and you will be found.
Good luck.
3301

Despite many fake Cicada puzzles (a 2017 contender is yet to be proved authentic), no new clues have been forthcoming and so the mystery continues.

There may be no definitive answer to Cicada. The Liber Primus may hold the key, but the key to what? And, why? For some this continues to remain a thrilling challenge; for others, it has lost its excitement, and there are still those who warn against the group: 'I was part of what you call 3301/Cicada for more than a decade, and I'm here to warn you: stay away.'

But since everything about Cicada 3301 is anonymous and secretive, there is no way of concluding what is real, who is behind the mysteries, or whether they are our salvation or our downfall. All we have left is The Liber Primus. The book is available to view on the web for all to decipher, so if you're interested maybe it's time to unearth your rune-book and start playing? Good Luck. JT

I was the walrus

The Gumtree ad that inspired a horror film

In June 2013, a bizarre advert appeared on the UK's free classifieds ads website Gumtree:

'I am looking for a lodger in my house. I have had a long and interesting life and have now chosen Brighton as a location for my retirement. Among the many things I have done in my life is to spend three years alone on St Lawrence Island. These were perhaps the most intense and fascinating years of my life and I was kept in companionship with a walrus whom I named Gregory. Never have I had such a fulfilling friendship with anyone, human or otherwise, and upon leaving the island I was heartbroken for months.

I now find myself in a large house overlooking Queen's Park and am keen to get a lodger. This is a position I am prepared to offer for free on the fulfilment of some conditions. I have, over the last few months been constructing a realistic walrus costume, which should fit most people of average proportions and allow for full and easy movement in character. To take on the position as my lodger you must be prepared to wear the walrus suit for approximately two hours each day. Whilst in the walrus costume you must be a walrus – there must be no speaking in a human voice and any communication must entail making utterances in the voice of a walrus. I believe there are recordings available on the web …

Other duties will involve catching and eating fish that I will occasionally throw to you whilst you are being the walrus. With the exception of this, you will be free to do whatever you choose and will have a spacious double room, complete run of the house … I am a considerate person to share a house with, and other than playing the accordion my tastes are easy to accommodate. Please contact me if you have any questions.'

Four hundred people applied for the room. Within a week, the position was declared to be filled. It wasn't long before the advert

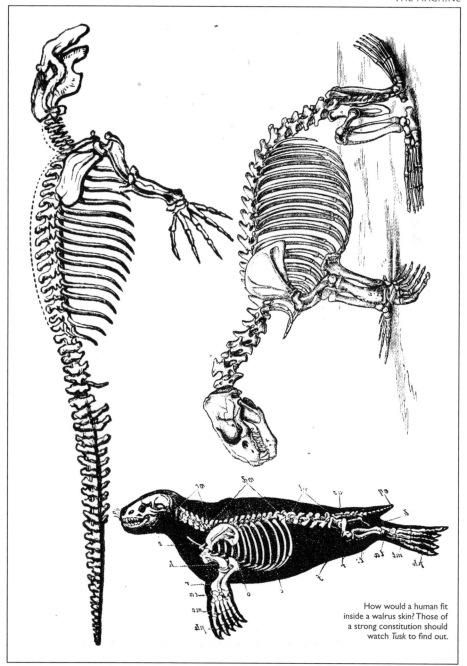

How would a human fit
inside a walrus skin? Those of
a strong constitution should
watch *Tusk* to find out.

went viral. It wormed its way through Twitter and finally reached the attention of film director Kevin Smith, who made it the topic of conversation for his 259th episode of *Smodcast* – the podcast he co-hosts with best friend and producer Scott Mosier. Despite the pair's giggling stoner ramblings, it is clear that Smith takes the advert seriously.

'He's clearly got issues but he sounds like a sweetheart,' Smith comments. 'Let's take bets. Does it end well for the tenant? Of course not. Imagine being trapped in this thing. I can see him being sewn into his walrus suit, elbows attached to his ribcage. This is a fucking horror film.'

The seed sown, Smith and Mosier begin to joke about the practicalities of making such a film. 'Four million dollars and we've got *The Walrus and the Carpenter*. The most expensive part of it would be the suit. I'm going with John Cusack as the lodger ...' giggles Smith.

After the podcast, Smith couldn't leave the idea alone. He puts the question to his followers: '#walrusyes if you want me to make this movie', he tweets, '#walrusno if you don't'. The response was overwhelmingly positive. Smith penned the script in 20 days and, in November that year, *The Walrus and the Carpenter* went into production.

Ten months later, in September 2014, the newly-titled *Tusk* premiered at the Toronto International Film Festival to reasonably good reviews. It begins with the story of two men, Wallace Bryton and Teddy Craft, hosting a podcast that makes fun of weird viral internet stories. Craft ends up investigating a strange room-to-let advert and gets more than he bargained for when he unwittingly becomes the successful applicant. *Tusk* divided Smith's followers. It was a departure for the director – best known for his slacker comedies – and was inevitably loved by some; dismissed as an over-stretched idea by others.

I WAS THE WALRUS

But while *Tusk* was creeping out viewers, the previous year a different comedy-horror show had been playing out in Brighton. For those who don't know it, Brighton has something of a reputation for eccentricity. It is a town with a fake Indian palace slap bang in the centre (the Royal Pavilion). A local cult, Thee Temple ov Psychick Youth, once formed a giant circle around the building in an attempt to levitate it, before Police shooed them away. Walk through Brighton in your birthday suit and few heads will turn; it's that kind of town. However strange messages in Brighton's small ads were indeed becoming the talk, not just of the town, but the national media.

A month prior to the Gumtree ad, another anonymous message had appeared on Brighton Council's Fix My Street website. It read:

'I was recently walking my affenpinscher around the Hanover area of Brighton when I noticed that a wormhole or vortex has opened up on Montreal Road. On closer inspection it seems to be some kind of portal to other times, places and dimensions. I would have investigated further but I was concerned my little dog would be sucked into it. At first I believed it might be part of the Brighton Festival but I believe it could be a hazard to the general public. I look forward to your response.'

Over the next few days, the complainant expanded on the unusual occurrence; the wormhole was now emitting an 'unsettling yellow

Chris Parkinson's artwork depicting the wormhole on Montreal Road, Brighton.

'The time has come,' the Walrus said, 'To talk of many things: Of shoes and ships and sealing wax Of cabbages and kings'. John Tenniel's illustration for Lewis Carroll's wonderful poem *The Walrus and the Carpenter*.

light' and a large snake was emerging from the wall (they included a picture). If a portal to another dimension was to appear anywhere in the UK, it would be Brighton. True to the spirit of the town, paranormal investigators turned up to locate the wormhole and local newspaper *The Argus* published the artist's impression of the serpent – just in case townsfolk couldn't picture the scene. The story made the national papers and even featured on the satirical BBC News programme, *Have I Got News For You*.

It was, of course, the calling card of the same trickster behind the Gumtree ad. Someone who would have kept his identity a secret had it not been for the surprising turn of events that led his prank to form the basis of a Hollywood movie. The very month of *Tusk*'s release, Smith and Mosier welcomed a special guest on to their podcast – **the culprit Chris Parkinson**, a Brighton poet and trickster. Kevin Smith's own bizarre story of how he had been inspired by the viral advert had itself gone viral and wormed its way back to Parkinson, who confessed to uploading the walrus ad 'during a quiet day at the office' and promptly found himself being invited over to America during the production of the film.

Parkinson was given the role of associate producer on *Tusk*.

As inspiration for a movie it was bizarre, although not unique. The previous year, the sci-fi time-travel comedy *Safety Not Guaranteed* had been conceived via a spoof classified ad from a 1997 edition of *Backwards Home* magazine: 'Wanted: Somebody to go back in time with me. This is not a joke. PO Box 91 Ocean View, WA 99393. You'll get paid after we get back. Must bring your own weapons. Safety not guaranteed. I have only done this once before.'

What makes *Tusk* unique, however, is that – thanks to Smith and Scott's dope-fuelled flights of fancy – podcast listeners were party to the mysterious creative process in which an idea is born, teased, sculpted and suddenly takes on a life of its own. It's also apparent how chance factors – and a sprinkling of mischief – are crucial to the creative process.

A key element to *Tusk*'s success, Smith notes, was the immobility of the walrus costume. If it had been any other large mammal, the whole idea would have been too expensive and impractical. 'Your art begat my art,' Smith says to Parkinson on the podcast, with a wry laugh. 'Good job I didn't settle on a rhinoceros then,' Parkinson replies, 'I did consider it.' DB

SEEKERS' DIRECTORY

Slenderman

DOCUMENTARY *Beware the Slenderman* (2017): This HBO documentary chronicles the tragic true-life story of Morgan Geyser and Anissa Weier who, after becoming obsessed with the internet phenomenon Slenderman, stabbed their friend 19 times. Viewer discretion is advised.

John Titor

FILM Enjoy a classic time-travelling film. Here are two corkers that often get overlooked. *Primer* (2014, directed by Shane Carruth) is about the accidental discovery of time travel and is one of the strangest, most complex and mind-bending time-travel films to date. At the heart of the film sits complex issues of science, technology and philosophy; in short, this film is a must-see. *La Jetée* (1962, directed by Chris Marker), is an elegant mix between an apocalyptic tomorrow's world, a post-structural art piece and a heartfelt love story. This seminal French New Wave short film was also the inspiration for Terry Gillam's *12 Monkeys*.

ACTIVITY Build a time machine and get in touch with us before this book is written – like this person did. rosycarricktimetraveller.blogspot. co.uk – and, if you're successful, we'll leave a cryptic time-travel credit to you at the back of the book.

Who is Satoshi Nakamoto?

INTERVIEW A California man named Dorian Prentice Satoshi Nakamoto denies having anything to do with Bitcoin, while being plied with plates of sushi: bit.ly/MysteriumDorianNakamoto

DOCUMENTARY *The Blockchain and Us* (2017). Economist and filmmaker Manuel Stagars explores Bitcoin and the blockchain through interviews with software developers, cryptologists, researchers, entrepreneurs, consultants, VCs, authors, politicians and futurists from around the world: blockchain-documentary.com

The Deep Web

BOOK *The Dark Net* (2015). A revelatory look at the depths of the digital world that sits at our fingertips. Follow journalist Jamie Bartlett through today's encrypted networks and dangerous online subcultures.

DOCUMENTARY *Deep Web: The Untold Story of Bitcoin and the Silk Road* (2015). Directed by Alex Winter, this documentary takes a hard look at the events surrounding the rise of Silk Road, the politics of decentralized cryptocurrencies and even features narration from Bitcoin enthusiast and all around nice guy, Keanu Reeves.

Cicada 3301

ACTIVITY Solve Liber Primus and discover who is behind the shadowy underworld of the Cicada 3301 mystery. If you do, you'll let us know, won't you?

I was the walrus

PODCAST Listen to the conversation that started it all – Smodcast Episode 259: The Walrus and the Carpenter: bit.ly/MysteriumSmodcast259

FILM *Tusk* (2013) is another instalment from the stoner comedy veteran Kevin Smith. The film follows a US podcaster (Justin Long) who journeys to meet a Canadian man with a dark Walrus-esque secret. According to Smith, the entirety of the music budget was blown on getting permission to use Fleetwood Mac's 'Tusk' for the film.

POETRY Stay up-to-date with the antics of Brighton's performance artist and poet Chris Parkinson, cdparkinson.wordpress.com. Current interests include the eating habits of politicians, tapirs and the history of the British press.

CHAPTER THREE

are we not human?

Prince Philip

Melanesian Volcano God

On Tanna, Prince Philip is considered to be a 'household god'. Such gods are acknowledged as having human characteristics and flaws – Philip, for example, is believed to be arrogant and flirtatious. His particular role is as a garden god, whose placation permits a good harvest of crops. Unlike the residents of Summer Isle in the film *The Wickerman*, this doesn't require the slow roasting of a policeman.

As the last reported case of cannibalism on the Melanesian island of Tanna was way back in 1969, visitors really have nothing to worry about these days. Unless they happen to be the Queen of England. While Tanna's residents acknowledge the Queen to be a powerful woman, her status pales in comparison to her husband; two of Tanna's tribes believe Prince Philip to be **the son of a local volcano god** and worship him accordingly. A battered, 30-year-old biography, signed photos of the Prince and a coronation-themed biscuit tin have pride of place in the hut of chief Seko from the Yaohnanen tribe – all treated with the same reverence as holy relics.

Daily prayers directed to the Prince are conducted using old-fashioned telephones, fashioned from creeper vines. Despite also being known as *man blong missis kwin* ('man belonging to Mrs Queen'), the Prince would rule supreme on Tanna. Being Lois Lane to Philip's Superman, the Queen, on the other hand, would need to be rather vigilant of local protocol.

> 'If the queen accompanies (The Prince), she must be careful not to see him drinking kava because if she does the local rules insist that she be executed summarily and on the spot with a single blow to the head with a giant root. If she does not accompany him, the Duke will be allocated three wives bearing a dowry of pigs and pillows. …Understandably perhaps, the Prince has never paid them a visit.'
> Tim Heald, *The Duke: A Portrait of Prince Philip*
> (Hodder & Stoughton, 1991)

To understand how and why Philip became a god on a remote island in the South Pacific (and one that he'd never even stepped foot on) we need a little context, history and a sprinkling of geography.

Tanna is one of 80 islands forming the archipelago Vanuatu in the South Pacific. Its inhabitants number around 30,000. In the centre of the island sits an active volcano, Yasur, revered as a god. Many of

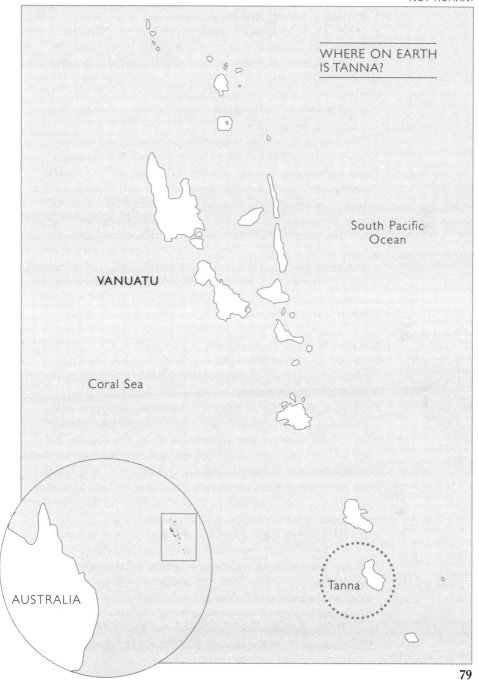

WHERE ON EARTH
IS TANNA?

South Pacific
Ocean

VANUATU

Coral Sea

AUSTRALIA

Tanna

Tanna's tribes still live traditionally in bamboo huts. Dress code for the tribes is an exercise in minimalism; just grass skirts for the women, while the men are naked save for their nambas – straw codpieces that keep the member pointing skywards. Hundred-day circumcision rituals – involving sticking flotsam and jetsam in the wound – leave every teenager's penis unique and highly 'customized'. The local brew – kava – **is a vision-inducing root**, whose revolting appearance is matched only by its creation.

Life wasn't always so for the people of Tanna. After French and English missionaries turned up uninvited in the late 18th century, Tanna's inhabitants were forced to wear clothes, curb the kava and cavorting, and convert to Christianity or risk death. Why they needed to hide their nakedness from an all-seeing God baffled them. As did the story of Jesus – if his followers had waited 2000 years for his return and he still hadn't materialized, surely he was not up to the job? Far from 'civilizing' the Tannese, the missionaries lasting legacy was – inadvertently – to kill many of them through the spread of Western diseases, many of which lay dormant in the clothes they insisted they wore. Understandably, the Tannese are **wary of the French and English**. The Americans however, are a different matter entirely.

JESI KRIS NO COME; JOHN FRUM HE COME

First arriving in the 1930s, US troops became a permanent fixture on Tanna during the Second World War, building airfields, hospitals and other military installations. Unlike the missionaries (who had finally given up and left by now), the Americans didn't care what the islanders practised or how they dressed and treated them as equals. The Tannese were particularly impressed to see white- and black-skinned men mixing together also as equals. Not only did the islanders get their dignity, nambas and kava back, they were delighted to be given food, Coca-Cola and other supplies, and were agog at the Americans futuristic machinery and vehicles. Much of what they saw would have been indistinguishable from magic. And they couldn't get enough of spam which – allegedly – reminded them of human flesh.

When the Americans returned home a few years after the war, they had made such a lasting impression on the islanders that two cults sprang up in their wake – Tom Navy and John Frum. The missionaries had promised Jesus would come; he never did. But Americans had. The name John Frum is believed to derive from soldiers introducing themselves to the islanders. With John being a common name, 'Hi, I'm John from …' became John Frum. Like the mythical Joe Bloggs,

Kava is prepared through the slow chewing of a pepper plant root, usually by the older ladies or younger men in the tribe. Once ready, it is spat into a bowl and mixed with water, ready for drinking. David Attenborough, faced with drinking a bowl during one of his trips to Melanesia did all he could to swallow it down without vomiting. When asked if he liked kava by the chief, Attenborough replied, 'Yes, really delicious.' 'Oh! Excellent!' roared the chief, 'pour him another bowl!'

The form of pidgin spoken on Tanna is Bislama, an English-based creole containing less than 500 words. As such, *rubber blong fak-fak* translates as 'condom', *bugarup* means 'broken', *kwin lisbet* is 'queen' and *handbag* is unspeakably rude.

John Frum was the archetypal everyman, transformed by the Tannese into a demigod.

Over the years, the John Frum cult developed elaborate rituals to encourage **the return of John and his cargo**. Every year on 15 February (John Frum Day) followers march around the island in homemade uniforms, clutching rifles made from bamboo. They even build extraordinary fetishes – life-size bamboo planes and lookout towers in which men talk to fake radio sets. Down on the makeshift runway, men wave cones to imaginary planes while other tribesmen sit all along the edges of the runway, day and night, watching the skies in the hope of luring back their god.

Why? As far as they could see the Americans who turned up weren't themselves making the stuff – planes, radios, food – that they were using. Instead, they were involved in all sorts of rituals, marching and dressing up. The Tannese figured that if they indulged in the same rituals, these would bring the return of the planes and food.

'Cargo cults' originated in Melanesia following encounters with Western civilization and advanced technology. Tribes perform rituals -- such as building runways for aeroplanes -- in the belief that they will herald the arrival of material wealth or 'cargo'.

MAN BLONG MRS QUEEN

Proud men of Tanna pose with photos of Prince Philip.

No one is entirely sure whether the US soldiers were the catalyst for the cult of John Frum or whether it already existed decades earlier through a kava-induced visionary myth. The same can be said for the

cult of Prince Philip. It is believed to have sprung up after the Prince and Queen visited Vanuatu (but not Tanna) in 1974; other evidence suggests it may have begun earlier. What we know for sure is that The Yaohnanen and a neighbouring tribe still worship Philip as a garden god and believe he is originally from Tanna. After all, a local legend had long decreed that a pale-skinned man would be created from the union of two women, emerge from Yasuo (the active volcano), travel and marry a woman of great power.

When two of Tanna's chiefs – Jack and Tuk – met Prince Philip during a visit to the Vanuatu in 1974, learned his history and discovered that he wasn't from Britain, it made sense that he could be their garden god incarnate. When Philip was later sent a nai-nai (a weapon for walloping pigs) as a gift from the villagers, he insisted on posing a hundred times with the object, in the hope that one photo would show him holding it correctly. It did the trick, when the islanders were sent the right photo, it added yet more evidence that he was a native of Tanna.

Since the 1970s, the tribes awaited the return of 'Pilip', believing that he would return on his 89th birthday (10 June 2010) as prophesied. In 2007, five members of the Yaohnanen's neighbouring tribe were invited to take part in a British reality TV show, *Meet the Natives*. It did little to quell the rivalry that already existed between the two Philip-worshipping tribes. When the men returned a few weeks later, having met the Prince in person, they brought round a few photos to their Yaohnanen neighbours as proof, gloated and passed on the message that the Prince said 'Hi'. It was bound to sting. While the prince failed to materialize on his 89th birthday as hoped, an 18-year-old Scottish student, living on the island as part of an exchange program, did a heroic job in explaining to both chiefs that Philip was very old, had many important duties at home but would be very much there in spirit.

The spirit of Philip is as strong on Tanna today as it ever was. He is still prayed to every day, his photos and other ephemera are kept in the chief's hut and he even features in the school curriculum as one of their gods who happens to live in a big house in England. What the Tannese would make of David Icke's claim that certain members of the British royal family are actually descended from a race of shape-shifting reptilians from the Draco constellation is anyone's guess. And, perhaps, a story for future pages of *The Mysterium*. DB

Uriel

The woman who fell to Earth

Mrs Ruth Norman was rather fond of beginning her sentences with 'As you Earth people say ...' And let's be honest, if you'd seen her wardrobe, who'd have thought she was anything other than a being from another world (namely the spiritual planet of Aries). After becoming consciously aware that her higher self was Archangel Uriel, in 1973 Ruth chose to go by that name, favouring gold and purple capes, tiaras, glitter and a heroic dollop of make-up. Most of the time she looked like a cross between Mrs Slocombe from *Are Your Being Served* (circa 1976) and a female Time Lord from *Dr Who*, which is of course no bad thing. Her most flamboyant outfit was a Ming the Merciless affair, into which were sewn bauble-like planets; around her throat was a giant flaming sun and into her headdress were woven fairy lights. She looked terrific.

Born in 1900 as a human, Norman co-founded the **Unarius Academy of Science** in the mid-1950s with her husband, Ernest. Along with their unique fourth-dimensional science of life teachings, the pair **believed the Chinese were originally from Mars** and that the spiritual plane of Venus was inhabited by beings composed of energy and light.

The initial mission of the Normans was to provide a higher spiritual understanding of life for the betterment of humankind. In 1973, after communicating with beings on other planets known as the Space Brothers, the Academy began to make preparations for the imminent arrival of 33 spaceships. It also pioneered past-life therapy for Earthlings. Uriel and Ernest were enthusiastic believers in past lives. Ruth came to believe that she had once been Mary of Bethany (Jesus' betrothed) and wrote about it in her catchily titled: *My 2000–year Psychic Memory as Mary of Bethany – 13th Disciple to Jesus of Nazareth*.

Inevitably, husband Ernest discovered himself to have been Jesus in a previous life too, while another Unariun found out he'd been Archangel Lucifer. Ruth went on to unearth many more of her own past lives and encouraged pupils to do the same. There were bonus

Unarius is an acronym for Universal Articulate Interdimensional Understanding of Science.

Ernest Norman had communications in 1955 with a Martian guide who gave him a tour of the underground cities of Mars and informed him that the Chinese were Martian descendants who visited Earth and intermixed with the natives: 'Martians are much older in soul evolution than the Eartheans. They are a quiet, peace loving people ... and came to this earth and started a colony, but they found it impractical to maintain. Nur El [the Martian guide] explained that this colony became our Chinese race through the evolution of time.' Ernest Norman: An Eyewitness Account *The Truth About Mars*, (Unarius Academy of Science Publications, 1998).

In 1979, Ruth Norman announced a spiritual promotion: she was no longer an archangel but a 'Lord of the Universe'.

Uriel's preferred mode of transport sported a 3D model of a UFO on the roof.

points for anyone recalling past lives as aliens or famous historical figures; it was the perfect opportunity for the Academy to build exotic stage sets for what would become Uriel's lasting legacy – her celluloid wonders.

PROPHESIES, PAGEANTRY AND PSYCHODRAMA

As well as her flamboyant attire and car – which had a 3D model of a saucer-shaped UFO perched on the roof – Uriel embraced technology. Through donations, the Academy was able to purchase film equipment while a warehouse building, adjacent to the main building of the Academy, was converted into a studio. Production began in the late seventies. The Academy was able to create their own creative films, devised theatrically to play out pupils' past lives through psychodrama as a means for healing. Pageantry, costume, art and drama – already woven into the everyday life of the Academy – were used to great effect.

Mixing the students' psychic memories of more 'technologically advanced civilizations', improvised theatre and Uriel's boundless enthusiasm, these technicolour mini-movies were saturated with colours and bizarre rituals that bring to mind the early short films of Kenneth Anger. At its peak in 2005, Unarius Academy of Science was broadcasting on 28 public access TV stations across the US. Even the titles were fantastic: *Lemuria Rising, The Decline and Destruction of the Orion Empire, A Visit to the Underground Cities of Mars*. Like The 1978 *Star Wars Holiday Special* they are best enjoyed from a distance.

After Uriel's death in 1993, a series of her predictions of alien arrivals – the biggest being in 2001 – left the group clearing their throats and avoiding eye contact as numbers dwindled. Or at least, that's how the outside world saw it. As far as the Academy was concerned, the Space Brothers didn't turn up because the people of Earth were not ready for such a contact – owing to the dire state of affairs across the planet. It seems doubtful then, we'll be seeing them anytime soon.

While there are fewer students attending classes at the Academy and participating in the day-to-day activities, it still has thousands of students worldwide, many of whom participate via live streaming. For those keen to sample its courses, details of activities and meetings can be found on their website. And before you ask, where else would they be based but California? DB

Rise of the Mirage Men

Keep watching the spies

In March 1950, at the University of Denver, Colorado, 90 science
students were asked to attend a presentation about flying saucers by
an anonymous lecturer. Word quickly spread around campus and on
the day of the talk, 8 March, the hall was filled to capacity. In the
50-minute presentation, the mysterious expert announced that not
only were flying saucers real, but that four of them had landed – not
crashed – on Earth, and three of them had been captured by the US
Air Force (USAF).

The lecturer described the saucers in some detail. They were:

> 'quite dissimilar to anything we have designed. There was not a
> rivet, nor a bolt, nor a screw in any of the ships … Their outer
> construction was of a light metal much resembling aluminium but
> so hard no application of heat could break it down. The discs … had
> revolving rings of metal, in the center of which were the cabins.'

But rather than being a normal university lecture, this felt more
like a market research exercise. Afterwards, attendees were asked
whether they believed what the presenter had told them; 60 per
cent said that they did, some of whom then found themselves
being questioned by Air Force intelligence officers. A follow-up
questionnaire was carried out among the students, by which point the
number who remained convinced had fallen from 60 to 50 per cent,
which was still considerably higher than the national average of 20 per
cent who believed that the flying saucers came from outer space – as
opposed to the more popular suggestions of Russia, or a secret US Air
Base. The message from the lecture was clear: exposure to a convincing
source of information, combined, no doubt, with a bit of peer pressure,
could encourage even the most pragmatic of college students to
believe the improbable.

The mysterious lecturer was later unmasked as a local salesman who
had fallen in with a known fraudster, perhaps unwittingly, perhaps not.

Their story made the national newspapers – and an FBI report – and then formed the basis of the first hugely successful UFO book, *Behind The Flying Saucers* (1950), by *Variety* magazine gossip columnist Frank Scully. All of this, however, only helped to perpetuate the nascent myth that flying saucers came from beyond our Earth and that the US government knew all about it, a myth that remains just as potent today.

About a month later, on 14 April 1950, the RAND Corporation, then the internal research and development arm of the USAF, published a top secret research paper entitled *The Exploitation of Superstitions for Purposes of Psychological Warfare*. The paper noted that 'superstitions flourish in an atmosphere of tension and insecurity' – much like the Cold War paranoia consuming America at the time – and asked 'what types of superstitious appeals will be best adapted to the various audiences to be propagandized?' By way of an answer, it suggested that 'a study of local superstitions as reflected in popular folklore might be profitable in providing answers to these questions'.

The presentation – announcing that UFOs were real – took place at the University of Denver, Colorado in 1950.

Echo was NASA's first communications satellite – a 100-foot shiny orb that went into orbit then reflected radio transmissions from one ground station back to another. Surely, this is exactly what you'd hope to find when searching for UFOs in Air Force hangars.

Had the students at Denver University just taken part in a propaganda experiment conducted by RAND and the USAF?

The RAND document outlines a number of successful deception gambits: how, in the 1920s, the British army broadcast 'the voice of God' from aeroplanes flying over Afghanistan's northwest frontier; and how, in both world wars, magic lantern images of Jesus and Mary were projected onto clouds to startle soldiers and civilians on the ground. It also describes the wartime activities of the English illusionist Jasper Maskelyne who describes how, in the Second World War, he and his men:

> 'were able to use illusions of an amusing nature in the Italian mountains ... In one area, they used a device which was little more than a gigantic scarecrow, about 12 feet high, and able to stagger forward under its own power and emit frightful flashes and bangs. This thing scared several Italian Sicilian villages ... and the inhabitants ... simply took to their heels for the next village, swearing that the Devil was marching ahead of the invading English ... Like all tales spread among uneducated folk (and helped, no doubt, by our agents), this story assumed almost unimaginable proportions.'

The RAND paper discusses the military potential for exploiting of beliefs about gods and devils, ghosts and monsters, astrology and magic, good luck charms, chain letters and more, but it curiously neglects to mention flying saucers, the biggest folkloric story of the day; one that was generating hundreds of newspaper stories and directly impacted on the USAF, whose job it was to investigate them. Was the author suffering from a severe case of saucer-blindness, or was there another reason for their omission?

MAINTAINING 'AMERICA'S CHARISMA ABROAD'

A year later, the Psychological Strategy Board (PSB) was signed into life by President Truman, many of whose documents remain secret to this day. Its role was to maintain 'America's charisma abroad', a job that required 'the control, procurement and production' of every conceivable means of transmitting ideas and information, from 'scholarly seminars, symposia, special tomes, learned journals [and] libraries, to church services, comic books, films, television and radio to folk songs, folklore, folk tales and itinerant storytellers.'

The PSB had allies and agents in many of the major media outlets:

its head was a former Time Life executive while the company's current boss, Henry Luce, was also a keen supporter, as was movie mogul Darryl Zanuck, the uncredited executive in charge of production on Robert Wise's 1951 classic *The Day the Earth Stood Still*. That film, released the year after Scully's book, suggested that alien visitors would be hard-working Christians, much like good Americans, and helped to project and promote America's role as global atomic policemen and guardian of world peace – just like its alien protagonist Klaatu.

AN EXTRATERRESTRIAL REBRAND?

After trying unsuccessfully to downplay the flying saucer problem, in April 1952, the USAF turned tack and announced, in a fully-sanctioned, several page article in America's favourite magazine, *LIFE* (with America's sweetheart Marilyn Monroe on the cover no less) that flying saucers were probably interplanetary in origin. Had someone at the Air Force decided to take the advice of its own RAND paper and make the flying saucers work for them? And how convenient it was that *LIFE*, an outlet very supportive of the aims of the Psychological Strategy Board, was there to aid them in their extraterrestrial rebranding of the saucer problem. Given that the flying saucers were now a popular obsession for millions of Americans, it was perhaps deemed healthier for them to believe that the discs were flown by friendly humanoid aliens like Klaatu, than it was for them to blab about secret US military aircraft, or to stir up panic about a Soviet saucer invasion.

If the USAF / *LIFE* article's intention was to get everyone watching the skies that summer, they did a great job. The US media was absolutely flooded with UFO reports and, over two nights in July – in scenes eerily reminiscent of *The Day The Earth Stood Still* – Washington DC was invaded by UFOs. But these saucers were only clearly visible on civilian and military radar screens, and seemed so adept at evading military jet interceptors that one of the radar operators was convinced that the UFOs were eavesdropping on their conversations.

General Sanford, the head of Air Force intelligence – who soon afterwards became chief of the supersecret National Security Agency – was particularly dismissive of the Washington flybys, but he couldn't dampen the nation's enthusiasm for saucer sightings. The incidents made the global news, drawing the largest press conference the Pentagon had seen since WWII.

As things began to look like they might get out of hand, the CIA

A 'flying saucer'
photographed over
Passaic, New Jersey
in 1952, documented
on the CIA website.

entered the story, and at the end of 1952 convened a secret meeting
to discuss the ramifications of the UFO problem. Known as the
Robertson Panel, the group of scientists and military intelligence
operatives decided that, while the UFOs themselves seemed to present
no 'direct physical threat to national security', the reporting of them

93

did, 'clogging ... channels of communication by irrelevant reports' and creating a cry wolf situation that could generate so many false alarms that genuine hostile actions by the Soviets might be ignored. What's more, the general interest in the subject threatened to inculcate 'a morbid national psychology in which skilful hostile propaganda could induce hysterical behaviour and harmful distrust of duly constituted authority'. To sum up, flying saucers could make a rebel out of you, or worse, a Communist.

Throughout the 1950s, thanks to countless films, newsreels, comics, newspapers and magazine articles – all the areas noted for coverage by the PSB – UFOs became as successful an American cultural export as the hula hoop or the frisbee. We see them starting to appear anywhere that the US had political concerns and ambitions, with Europe and Latin America – both key psychological battlegrounds in the cultural war against Communism – being particularly affected.

This sequence of events charts the rise of the Mirage Men. These are the disinformation specialists working within America's military intelligence apparatus who, for the past 70 years, have shaped and manipulated popular ideas about UFOs to create a useful cover for all manner of operations: from test flights of advanced secret aircraft, to labyrinthine psychological operations whose motivations are not immediately obvious to anybody on the outside.

Was there ever a dedicated programme to promote UFO beliefs? Possibly, but if so, it's unlikely that it existed for more than a few years – it may, for example, have been connected to the USAF's UFO investigation programme, Project Blue Book, which ran from 1952–1969. But such a dedicated programme wouldn't really be necessary: anyone who promotes ideas about ETs and UFOs is effectively part of the Mirage Man apparatus, whether they know it or not. Since the flying saucer brand went global in 1952, the UFO lore has enjoyed a vibrant life of its own, supported by a complex patchwork of believers, promoters, seekers and charlatans, all nourished by the sightings of thousands of new witnesses every year.

But the story is much older than that. While the UFO as we know and understand it is a creation of the Cold War, the UFOs themselves – which come in all shapes, colours and sizes – have been seen by humans since we first began to look up at the skies. In the past, we spoke of gods in fiery chariots, restless spirits, witches on broomsticks and winged angels, the mythic antecedents of today's extraterrestrials, zipping through the atmosphere in their anti-gravity vehicles. These stories are 20th and 21st century folklore, myths of our modern era –

the angels now have technology, but fulfil the same ancient role that they always have, to give humankind hope about its own future on Earth, and now in outer space.

THE ROLE OF MODERN MYTHOLOGY

This kind of myth-making is a human necessity; it's one of the things we do best. Myths are useful; they guide us and help us to make sense of the incomprehensible, those things and events too strange or complex for us to understand. They provide emotionally satisfying answers to difficult questions: how did we get here? Why is the world like it is? Why are we at war with people who were once our friends? Why did the World Trade Center collapse? Where do UFOs come from?

Over the decades, this ET mythology has begun to take on the tenets of a religion. There are, after all, water molecules on Mars and the Moon, while new Earth-like planets are being found every year. It can only be a matter of time before we find something that we can all recognize as life elsewhere in the universe – and if advanced forms of life do indeed prove to have visited us, it might be quite sensible to worship it, or at least ask it some polite questions.

We may not yet have proof that ET visitors are real, but we do know that the Mirage Men are, and we don't have to look very far to find evidence of their power. In recent years we've seen their work manifest in news reports of strange lights over Iran's burgeoning nuclear programme, while the following April 2010 news report from Pakistan's *The Nation* demonstrates that the lore is very much alive. New myths are evolving in the Middle East surrounding America and the UK's own UFOs – the unmanned drones used to devastating effect in distant combat zones. A survivor of a drone attack on an Afghan village told a reporter: 'The drones are not material creatures. Actually, they are spiritual beings. They don't need earthly runways for taking off … They live in outer space, beyond the international boundaries of Afghanistan and Pakistan. When they feel hungry, they swoop down and kill innocent Afghani women and children. They eat the corpses and fly back to their special residences for a siesta. When they again feel hungry, they again swoop down and kill another lot of innocent women and children. Having devoured the dead bodies, they fly back to their bedrooms in space. It has been going on and on like this for years.' MP

The inimitable Chuck Tingle

Enter the bizarre world of the 'Tingler'

Meet Alex and Keith. Alex is a lone, nervous traveller on a passenger plane, experiencing some heavy turbulence. Keith is … the plane. They chat, bond and Keith opens up about his loneliness, despite being a highly successful international card shark. Later, they meet at Keith's mansion. Alex smears sunscreen over Keith's smooth, metallic body and they have fantastic sex.

I'm Gay For My Living Billionaire Jet Plane is a classic 'Tingler' – part of an ever-growing body of niche gay erotic fiction by Chuck Tingle. Self-publishing through Amazon, the pseudonymous author started by penning stories about encounters with dinosaurs and unicorns, before moving on to anthropomorphized objects and even concepts. Early Tinglers include *Taken by the Gay Unicorn Biker* and *Pounded by President Bigfoot*; a later story is entitled *Slammed in the Butthole by My Concept of Linear Time*. 2015 saw the release of *Pounded in the Butt by my Own Butt*. This was swiftly followed by *Pounded in the Butt by My Book 'Pounded in the Butt by My Own Book'*. And yes, it later became a trilogy.

Chuck's inevitable cult following is founded not just on his bizarre writing style – which could be read as a satire on badly written erotica – but on his creation of an even more surreal public persona. Through his Twitter feed, website and interviews, Tingle has revealed himself to be a Tae Kwon do grandmaster with a PhD in holistic massage at DeVry University (which does not offer such a degree). He lives with his son and carer Jon in Billing, Montana, and enjoys chocolate milk and a big spaghetti breakfast. Despite tens of thousands of followers on Twitter, Tingle only follows Taylor Swift and is prone to including such random hashtags as #the and #its. His fans – known as buckaroos – have, on the whole, taken the whole thing as a joke.

Any public appearances only add to the intrigue. In 2016 – two years

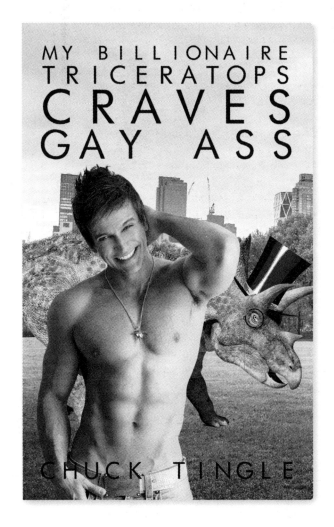

MY BILLIONAIRE
TRICERATOPS
CRAVES
GAY ASS

CHUCK TINGLE

Jeremy was never
quite sure about his
feelings for Oliver, his
gay pet dinosaur, until
Oliver scores big
and leaves home to
pursue his dreams
of being a dancer.

after his first book was released – Tingle dipped his toes into the world
of podcasts, giving a live interview on the UK's *Ian Boldsworth Show*
on Fubar Radio, during which Boldsworth and Tingle undertook a
lengthy conversation about the practicalities of having sex with a tree.
Tingle is gentle and thoughtful throughout; his voice carries a slow
whimsical drawl, reminiscent of the comedian Emo Philips. That same
year, after an in-depth phone interview with Tingle on *Smart Bitches*,

Chuck Tingle
embraces the
adult colouring
book trend.

Trashy Books, host Sarah Wendell allegedly claimed she was none the wiser as to whether Tingle was a comic character or a real person.

Tingle's voice can also be heard on his self-titled YouTube channel, in which a man in a white tae kwon do suit leads meditations with

ARE WE
NOT HUMAN?

a paper bag on his head. Discrepancies between the voice heard on YouTube and the podcasts only adds to the confusion. Are one or both of these an imposter? Is Tingle the creation of more than one person?

While perplexing and delighting thousands, Tingle does have his detractors. Some profess to find the backstory, told by his son, that Chuck is an autistic savant with schizophrenic tendencies, to be in rather poor taste. For the most part though, Tingle's world is one of overwhelming positivity. A common philosophical theme running through his books is an unashamed belief in the transformative power of love, even if it is with inanimate objects. In *Turned Gay By The Living Alpha Diner*, Tingle's trucker protagonist writes, 'For some reason, I find myself looking away, slightly taken aback by the restaurant's confident demeanour.' The story ends with a position opening up at the diner and the pair live happily ever after.

While Tingle's self-referential titles get ever more playful, whoever is behind the character has started to show his political leanings. In 2016, the author became the centre of a controversy. His short story 'Space Raptor Butt Invasion', was nominated for a Hugo Award for Best Short Story. For a number of years, the prestigious awards for science fiction and fantasy literature have been hijacked by bigoted trolls, irritated by the judge's efforts to improve ethnic and gender diversity in its nominees. In mobilizing the vote for Tingle, alt-right group Rabid Puppies took great delight in an action they saw as discrediting the Hugos. That's when Chuck decided to step in.

Tingle bought the domain name therabidpuppies.com, filled it with messages of love (in Tingle's own unique style), sent anti-harassment activist – and arch-nemesis of the puppy trolls – Zoe Quinn in his place to the awards and rushed out a new story: 'Slammed in the Butt By My Hugo Nomination'. The plot is a work of meta-comic genius, narrated by Chuck's reverse twin, Tuck Bingle, who accidentally gets sent Chuck Tingle's award nomination. Bingle shares his realization that he is a character in an alternative universe known as The Tingleverse, comprised of different layers: 'the lower it gets, the gayer it becomes' until one reaches the Tingularity. The story ends, as you might guess, with Bingle having sex with the award.

Trump, Brangelina, the presidential election and even quantum physicist Erwin Schrödinger have featured in Tingle's rapidly growing body of work, while its ongoing meta-narrative, surreal humour and social commentary prevent his books from being merely a one-trick pony. 'Chuck Tingle is the greatest author of our generation', states the banner headline on his website. Who are we to argue? DB

SEEKERS' DIRECTORY

Prince Philip

BOOK *The Bald Trilogy: Furtive Nudist, Pigspurt* and *Jamais Vu* (1995). Three one-man shows by Ken Campbell compiled into one volume. The third, *Jamais Vu*, spins a seditious yarn about going in search of the tribes who consider Prince Philip to be a god. Campbell was a performer, comic, theatre director and creative powerhouse from the 1960s until his death in 2008. For a playful introduction to his life and works, pick up a copy of our first book, *The Odditorium* (2016).

JOURNAL Described by the *Independent* as 'one of the most weirdly beautiful, beautifully weird magazines of the past hundred-odd years', *Strange Attractor*, edited by *The Mysterium* contributor Mark Pilkington, is a marvellous and rather meaty journal that delves into the fringes of knowledge, culture and belief. Volume one includes a long read about 'The Last Cargo Cult'. strangeattractor.co.uk

DOCUMENTARY *The People of Paradise: Cargo Cult* (1960). This BBC documentary in which a young David Attenborough interviews members of the John Frum cargo cult, is essential viewing. Being early Attenborough, you might need to forgive him for describing a piece of artwork by Tanna's residents as 'childlike and pathetic' – he was young, brash and probably on a kava-comedown. bit.ly/ MysteriumCargoCult

The Fantastic Invasion John Frum and USA (1991) is an unusual documentary from the BBC that describes the origins and evolution of the John Frum cargo cult on Tanna.

Meet the Natives (Channel 4, 2007) is a compelling documentary. It follows the experiences of five men from Tanna, who stay with hosts in the UK and experience three tiers of the British class system. Along the way, they try out trampolining, wash down their KFC with Vimto and try not to look perplexed when given Eccles cakes as a ceremonial gift.

Uriel

WORKSHOP Discover your past lives on other planets through a workshop with the Unarius Society: unarius.org

BOOK Dive into the magical and mystical world of Uriel by reading *Exploring the Universe with Starship Voyager* (1986), written by Ruth E. Norman and Charles Spaegel, a hefty tome that runs an even heftier price because of its scarcity. The catchily titled *My 2000 Year Psychic Memory: Mary of Bethany – 13th Disciple to Jesus of Nazareth* (1987), Ruth E. Norman, is pricey too.

DOCUMENTARY *Unarius: We Are Not Alone* (2016). A glimpse into the group's exuberant, radically benevolent leader Ruth E. Norman, aka Archangel Uriel. Uriel took her ambitious collective of students on a quest to explore the mysteries of the universe and achieve personal transformation by producing a film library of wildly imaginative psychodramas. Prized by collectors for years, they are some of the most mind-blowing examples of outsider cinema: thefront.com/watch/we-are-not-alone/

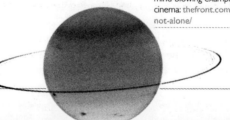

Rise of the Mirage Men

DOCUMENTARY For over 60 years, teams within the US Air Force and Intelligence services manipulated beliefs about UFOs and ET visitations as part of their counterintelligence programmes. In doing so they spawned a mythology so powerful that it captivated and warped many brilliant minds, including several of their own. *Mirage Men* (2013) delves deeper into a myth that took over the world.

The inimitable Chuck Tingle

BOOKS The subversive, niche, gay pornographic writings of Chuck Tingle are also a work of surreal and comic genius. Here are few choice cuts from the Tingle canon:

Slammed in the Butt by the Living Leftover Chocolate Chip Cookies from My Kitchen Cabinet (2016). Possibly the only 'novel' that features sentient leftover cookies – the plot follows an overworked milk bar employee named Nick and his journey into a land of homoerotic sensuality. Perfect for a quiet evening in.

Slammed in the Butt by My Smartphone's Missing Headphone Jack (2016). Quite the Tingler. Join Relm – an IT marketer – who finds himself in a storm of sexy problems when the arrival of the new 'mePhone' has no headphone input.

Dr Chuck Tingle's Complete Guide to Film (2017). Well-known for his love of the fantastic and the artistic, the revered Dr Tingle takes us on a magical journey through the world of cinema. Oh Chuck, is there anything you can't do?

TWITTER Meet the man himself @chucktingle

strange sounds
& spooky transmissions

Ghost radio

Time to adjust your frequency

In the 1950s, amateur radio enthusiasts and cryptographers around the world began reporting mysterious transmissions on short wave. Long lists of numbers orated by synthesized female voices, snippets of music, gongs and eerie sounds were being broadcast on the hour every hour from dozens of unidentified locations across the globe.

Numbers stations, as they became known, each gained a moniker over the decades: Nancy Adam Susan, Bulgarian Betty, Russian Man, Spanish Lady, Yosemite Sam and The Swedish Rhapsody, to name but a few. One of the best-known, the Lincolnshire Poacher, began with a prelude – the quirky tune of the first verse of this old English folk song:

'When I was bound apprentice in famous Lincolnshire,
Full well I serv'd my master, for more than seven year,
Till I took up to poaching, as you shall quickly hear.
Oh, 'tis my delight on a shining night, in the season of the year.'

Most numbers stations follow a similar pattern. Transmissions begin and end with a short prelude, as a means of identifying the station. Preludes range from musical refrains to electronic sounds or simple words or phrases, such as '*Achtung!*'. The main body of each transmission comprises strings of numbers in groups of four or five digits, read by synthesized voices, lasting up to an hour. Some also use Morse Code or strange bleeps to get their mysterious messages across.

Theories abound as to what these numbers represent, from an elaborate hoax to communications from extraterrestrials. The most plausible is that Number Stations are used by intelligence agencies for transmitting one-way coded messages to secret agents. After all, in a 1950s household, radios were one of the few pieces of equipment that could be utilized by a spy without arousing suspicion.

But while short wave would seem to be a plausible means of transmitting secret code in the early days of the Cold War, wouldn't it

Sound mirrors near Dungeness in Kent, UK – concrete structures used to concentrate sound waves before the invention of radar.

seem unlikely that such an archaic system of communication would still be used today? Perhaps not. The benefits of using radio waves as one-way code are that, unlike computers and phones, they leave no trace on any device. Spies can write the numbers down, decode them, then burn, rip up or eat the evidence with a side order of fries. Recipients of these codes could be anywhere in the world and remain untraceable.

Allegedly, when Ceausescu's dictatorship in Romania collapsed in 1989, number station transmissions from the country promptly ceased, adding credence to the theory of Cold War spying. If this is the case however, no government agency across the world has ever admitted any responsibility for them. Fifty years after their discovery, Number Stations may be on the decline but they can still be found, broadcasting from Europe, the Middle East and America.

DIGITAL NUMBER STATIONS

Along with analogue Number Stations, a growing presence of bizarre codes can be found on YouTube and Twitter. One of the biggest YouTube mysteries of recent years was Webdriver Torso, a channel responsible for uploading hundreds of thousands of short abstract videos containing red and blue shapes and different sine wave tones.

Conspiracies abounded until Google broke the silence in 2014 and admitted to owning the account, citing it as a test channel to ensure quality control of the thousands of videos uploaded hourly on

THREE OF THE WEIRDEST NUMBER STATIONS

UVB-76

This Russian-based station transmits a repetitive buzzing noise for months – sometimes years – before the sound is momentarily broken by a Russian voice reading out numbers and names. Some theories suggest UVB-76 is associated with Russia's 'Dead Hand' nuclear control system – still believed to be operative – primed to automatically fire nuclear rockets at anyone the Russians see as a threat to world peace.

Yosemite Sam

Yosemite Sam first materialized in 2004, transmitting on four separate frequencies from Albuquerque, New Mexico. It began with a recording of Bugs Bunny's arch-nemesis yelling: 'Varmint, I'm going to blow you to smithereens'. Number codes were then heard in two-minute bursts, twice repeated. Sam disappeared a few months later, as mysteriously as he first appeared.

Yankee Hotel Foxtrot

Originating in Tel Aviv and believed to be the work of Mossad, this number station transmitted 24/7 from the 1960s to 2001, utilizing a woman's voice and the phonetic alphabet. It is best known for having given its name to the 2001 album by Wilco, which also included extracts of the woman's voice speaking the three words.

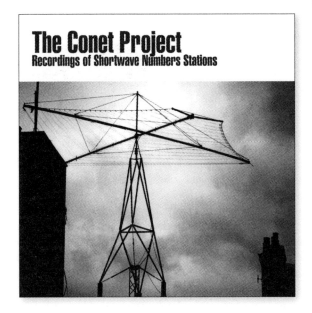

The Conet Project
Recordings of Shortwave Numbers Stations

YouTube. On Twitter, handles like @googuns and @xzv-94 regularly tweet coded number sequences, always ending with 000, suggesting that these are either spambots, spy messages or coded communication between members of a drug cartel. Odd phrases and gobbledygook messages regularly circulate the Twittersphere too. 'Iowa City schools ask state for an audit' – a minor story from the Iowa's Quad City Times in 2011 – continues to be retweeted for reasons unknown.

UK enthusiast, Akin Fernandez, has archived hundreds of recordings from numbers stations over the past 20 years and released selections of them in an audio collection titled The Conet Project. Many other obsessives continue to keep track of Number Stations – priyom.org and hfunderground.com have up-to-date information on the most active stations. The ethereal nature of these transmissions have led bands like Boards of Canada, Oddfellow's Casino and Stereolab to use samples of numbers stations on their music. They have featured in the podcast **Welcome to Night Vale** too. To listen to numbers stations, tune in between 2 Mhz and 26 Mhz on shortwave radio, where you'll hear them broadcast in Russian, Spanish, Chinese, German and English. To this day, we still can't be certain who is transmitting these coded monologues or why. More beguiling still, the codes remain unbreakable. *DB*

WZZZ is the local numbers station in Welcome to Night Vale, broadcast from a tall antenna at the back of an abandoned gas station on Oxford Street. A monotone female voice reads random numbers, interspersed with chimes, every hour and every day.

The Hum

Can you hear that?

What links the Ruskies, randy fish, a Rolls-Royce factory, wind farms, tinnitus, submarine communications, telephone wires and the end of the world? They have all – at some point – been blamed for one of the most enduring and bizarre phenomena of the last 50 years: a pervasive low-frequency vibration heard by tens of thousands of people in different locations across the globe. In the UK, The Hum has been reported everywhere from Grimsby to Aberdeen. Around the world, it has been heard in Canada, Spain, India, USA and New Zealand. The Hum is particularly pervasive in Taos, New Mexico, where roughly two per cent of the population have been suffering since 1991. This is a sound so pernicious it has allegedly even driven people to suicide. The baffling thing is – no one can be really sure if The Hum is a genuinely external phenomena.

Reports of a mysterious low-frequency vibration first began in the 1940s. By the 1970s, the Bristol Hum, heard by over 2000 residents, became global news. As similar stories came to light over the decades, the most troubled areas acquired the dubious honour of a moniker, hence Canada and the US now have the Taos Hum, Kokomo Hum, Ranchlands Hum and the Windsor Hum (which for residents of the UK could also be a royal faux pas). There should really be a Roman Hum but the Italians – not ones to follow the crowd – named theirs Ron Ron instead.

While some, such as Ron Ron, disappeared as mysteriously as they appeared a few months later, the Bristol and Taos Hum continue four decades on, to the frustration of a susceptible minority. Those afflicted describe the sound as a throb or constant vibration – akin to a distant diesel engine or lorry ticking over. Many complain that the sound affects their sleep and general wellbeing; more violent reactions include nosebleeds, nausea, headaches and even rattling teeth.

In some locations, The Hum can only be heard at night between specific hours, elsewhere it is a 24/7 phenomena. Many sufferers say it can be heard most clearly inside their homes and stationary cars;

double glazing and soundproofing only make it worse. For others, it can only be heard in specific locations in their town or city, ruling out the suggestion that it is a form of tinnitus. The fact that only a small percentage of people – largely middle-aged or older – can hear The Hum and only in certain areas makes it difficult to determine if it really is an external or internal problem. Low-frequency sounds can carry for many miles and are much harder to locate than high frequency.

POSSIBLE CAUSES OF THE HUM

Some theories suggest that The Hum is caused by electromagnetic waves emitted by the Earth's radiation belt (no, we're not really sure what that means either) or by the Aurora Borealis. Reports of The Hum in urban areas close to water have led some scientists to suggest that the pressure of seismic waves on the ocean floor is causing a low earthly rumble. Others theorize that vast movements of fish, shrimp and squid – emitting gas from their propel bladders – may be creating a great sub-bass fart. Male Midshipmen fish are also known to wake houseboat sleepers with their deep resonating grunts when trying to lure a female suitor. However, considering that Taos, New Mexico, where The Hum is particularly persistent, is over 1,000 km from the nearest coast, these theories are no more likely than the Hum being caused by Martians having a rave on the dark side of the moon, or the imminent return of Jesus (a genuine theory for some).

Only a small number of people appear to be susceptible to The Hum; it is also notoriously difficult to record low-frequency sounds. Could it actually be inside the heads of sufferers? After all, the human body is believed to generate a weak frequency of its own. Might this explain why some sufferers report the sound being more acute in sealed places – are they picking up their own 'bad vibes'? But that doesn't explain why so many cite specific times of day or night when it can be heard.

Recent reports in the UK of a 'hummadruz' (a cocktail of hum, drone, and buzzing) only add to the confusion. Is The Hum evolving, spawning mutant offspring, or is it simply the case that slowly and surely, our ears and brains are melting under the constant radiation from mobile phones? Hey, it's only a theory. Don't shoot the messenger. DB

THE HUM ACROSS THE UK

'Some nights we wake up with our hearts racing and my husband has felt his teeth shaking in his head.'
Adele Farquharson, Whitehills, Banffshire (6 May, 2001, *Sunday Telegraph*)

'If it happens during the winter then it is probably the phone lines contracting.'
Ian Moir, retired telephone engineer, Garthdee, Aberdeen
(19 February, 1999, *Aberdeen Evening Express*)

'It leaves a buzzing in your head for the rest of the day.'
Marylin Grech, Durham
(9 June, 2011, *The Guardian*)

Residents kept awake 12pm–4pm
Largs, North Ayrshire

'It gives you headaches, your ears pop, you feel your nose bursting and your chest crushing in.'
Georgie Hyslop, Largs, North Ayrshire (6 May, 2001, *Sunday Telegraph*)

'It's bloody annoying.'
Local resident, Leeds
(2007, Twitter)

'I live near a quarry, and I am used to a lot of noise, it's just that this particular kind of noise is driving me mad.'
Nan Griffiths, Minffordd nr. Porthmadog
(4 November, 2008, *Daily Post North Wales*)

More noticeable inside dwellings
Minffordd nr. Porthmadog

'The noise is constant and disturbing our sleep.'
Matthew Bennett, Barnwood, Gloucester
(3 July, 2009, *The Gloucester Citizen*)

'It's like a constant low-frequency rumble that you can't get away from. Ahhhhh!'
Owen Royal, Bristol
(17 January, 2016, Twitter)

'It's a really low-pitched sound that literally pulsates through the house.'
Maria Dennett, Sholing, Southampton, (24 October, 2013, *Independent*)

'I thought I was going mad at first. I hear it every night unless it's windy or raining.'
Linda Zammit, Woolston, Southampton (24 October, 2013, *Independent*)

110

The Portsmouth Sinfonia

Why did the world's worst orchestra throw in the towel?

In his popular book *Outliers* (2008), Malcolm Gladwell's explores an idea first presented by psychologist Anders Ericsson – that to become truly accomplished at something, such as playing the violin, we need to put in some serious hours' practice. For Gladwell, the magic number was 10,000 hours. Without this amount of practice, he claimed, all we can really expect is to be mediocre or, at worst, truly hopeless. And when it comes to the violin, there really is nothing more excruciating than bad playing. Yet, uniquely, a hugely popular group of musicians once existed for whom Gladwell's 'talent code' simply did not apply. In fact, it proved to be their very undoing.

It's the evening of 28 May 1974 and – at the pinnacle of their career – an orchestra prepare to perform to a sellout audience at The Royal Albert Hall. Backstage, the musicians are busily tuning their instruments; outside an assembled crowd of devoted fans chat with a documentary film crew, there to capture this momentous occasion. Among the crowd are two American visitors who confess: 'We aren't familiar with the orchestra but thought we might like it.'

When everyone is seated, conductor John Farley appears – suitably attired in tails and with a white carnation in his breast pocket – and is cheered on by the crowd. Brian Eno can be spotted among the musicians, wearing a red beret and clutching a clarinet. A respectable hush descends as Farley raises his baton and leads the orchestra in with their first piece, Strauss's *Also Sprach Zarathustra*. The strings began their low drone before the brass bursts in with the tune's familiar ascending five notes. It is utterly horrible. Sounds waver and collapse, trumpets squeal, trombones rasp. A caterwauling, cacophonous mess, it brings the audience to tears of laughter and ends with rapturous applause. The epic is followed by 'Dance of the

Sugarplum Fairy', delivered with the same naivety and clumsiness. The American visitors, utterly confused by the aural onslaught, vacate their seats. The rest of the audience continue to respond with giggles of encouragement.

During the Sinfonia's performance of Beethoven's *1812 Overture*, conductor John Farley suddenly remembers that his grandmother is in the audience and has a bad heart. Afraid that the cannons might send her over the edge, he frantically signals to the percussionist not to fire them. **Misinterpreting the conductor's waving**, the percussionist sets the cannons off and there a deafening blast that is definitely not where it's supposed to be in the music. Thankfully, Farley's grandmother lived to tell the tale.

At the end of the show, the Sinfonia are joined by a 300-strong choir for a rousing (if inebriated) version of 'Hallelujah' from Handel's *Messiah*. For The Portsmouth Sinfonia, the night is a triumph. So how did a shabby, amateur outfit come to play a sellout show at such a prestigious venue?

HAVE YOU GOT WHAT IT DOESN'T TAKE?

The Portsmouth Sinfonia was formed in 1970 by Gavin Bryars, then a lecturer in music at Portsmouth College of Arts. Inspired by the TV show *Opportunity Knocks* (an early version of *Britain's Got Talent*), Bryars ran a talent show over three days at his college and conceived his own idea for the competition: an orchestra composed entirely of members who had no prior skills on their chosen instrument.

Pre-empting the DIY punk ethos that anyone can form a band, Bryars' tempting advert for would-be members ran: 'Have you got what it doesn't take?' Offers flooded in and the Sinfonia was born. Those who joined were, however, expected to take it seriously and try their best: attendance at rehearsals was compulsory. When they began to perform live it wasn't long before they'd attracted a few famous members. As well as Bryars on cello, **composer Michael Nyman joined them on sousaphone**, Steve Beresford on trumpet and Brian Eno on clarinet.

By 1973, the ensemble had signed a record deal with Transatlantic Records. *Portsmouth Sinfonia Plays the Popular Classics* was produced by Eno, recorded in one take and included spirited versions of 'Hall of the Mountain King', 'Air', 'Jupiter' from the *Planet Suite*, Beethoven's Fifth and the William Tell Overture. A rebuttal from the BBC when the Sinfonia requested to play The Proms led to their manager Martin Lewis booking the Albert Hall himself. Hallelujah! The Portsmouth

The Sinfonia's conductor, John Farley, once famously led a count-in to 'The Blue Danube' waltz with a 1-2-3-4. Many members of the Sinfonia confessed they found it best to ignore him.

Nyman memorably joined the group halfway through one of their performances in London, after borrowing a cello.

Sinfonia at the Royal Albert Hall followed hot on its tail then, six year later, *20 Classic Rock Classics*, which included covers of '(I Can't Get No) Satisfaction', 'Bridge Over Troubled Water', 'Pinball Wizard' and a single, 'Classical Muddly', inspired by popular mash-up singles of the time.

The Sinfonia book-ended the 70s, serving as an enduring statement that classical music need not be elitist and poe-faced. It was a playful nod to Dadaism, surrealism and experimental art, an inclusive musical experiment at a time when both Classical and rock music could feel exclusive to those with the necessary background, money or skill. Not everyone however, shared this belief. *Rolling Stone* magazine gave *Portsmouth Sinfonia Plays the Popular Classics* a damning one star review, deeming it to be an elitist, intellectual joke. In creating a punk orchestra, **Bryars had broken one of the greatest taboos in the art world**: bringing humour to the avant-garde.

But why did the world's worst orchestra disappear? Rare footage of one of the group's last ever performances – an orchestral version of The Shadows' 'Apache' for a TV show – reveals Farley in a gold lame suit, now conducting *behind* the orchestra. The group's performance is ropey but passable. They disbanded shortly after. For some, the joke had worn too thin while many others felt unable to continue with the experiment for practical reasons. After ten years of rehearsals, recordings and live performances, slowly and surely each member of the group had been clocking up an impressive number of hours of practice. The Portsmouth Sinfonia had simply become too competent on their instruments. *DB*

2 February, 1975. Members of the Portsmouth Sinfonia give a concert at Wandsworth Prison, London.

Bryars remains a respected experimental musician. His most famous composition, 'Jesus Blood Never Failed Me Yet', is a 40-minute orchestral piece written around a loop of a few lines of a song Bryars heard a tramp singing in the street and captured on his recorder.

Space oddities

Strange transmissions from outer space

While we have yet to discover other intelligent alien life forms, could rogue signals from deep space offer evidence that the universe is not as a quiet as it appears? Here are three of the most enigmatic transmissions that have left some cosmologists to speculate that we might not be alone.

THE WOW! SIGNAL

In 1977, Jerry Ehman, a volunteer astronomer for the Search for Extraterrestrial Intelligence (SETI) at Perkin's Observatory, Ohio, noticed an anomalous transmission from the constellation of Sagittarius. For 72 seconds, a signal 30 times stronger than all background emissions was picked up by the radio telescope. Effectively a giant antenna, the telescope was tuned to frequencies closest to these emitted by hydrogen, thought to be **the most common and oldest thing in the universe**.

Science fiction writer Harlan Ellison was once quoted as saying 'the two most abundant materials in the universe are hydrogen and stupidity.'

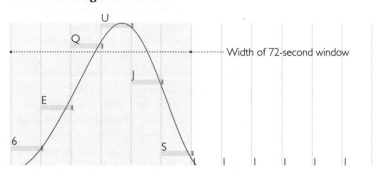

Width of 72-second window

Ehman's signal bore all the hallmarks of an anomaly outside of all known signals so far picked up from the universe. He was so overjoyed at discovering what he thought might be proof of extraterrestrial life that he wrote 'Wow!' in the margins of his computer printout. Despite continued searches, a repeat of the Wow! signal has never been detected. While some scientists have speculated as to whether Ehman had picked up the signal from one of two comets known to have been loitering in that constellation around that time, the Wow! remains as evidence of a genuine possibility that ETs might be out there, running their own cosmic radio show on Hydrogen FM.

THE 'GOSH I WONDER WHAT IT WAS?' TRANSMISSION

Nearly 40 years after the Wow! signal was first detected, a team of SETI astronomers based in Russia picked up another strong, rogue signal. This time it came from the vicinity of the star HD164595, 94 light years from Earth in the constellation Hercules. While HD164595 (let's call it Shirley from now on) is known to have an orbiting planet, roughly the same size as Neptune, this celestial body is so close to Shirley that temperatures alone would make the possibility of life there highly improbable, despite claims to the contrary.

Like the Wow! signal, this transmission also never repeated, leaving the SETI team to again speculate on its origins. Seth Shostak, senior astronomer at SETI said, in an interview for space.com, 'If SETI can't find it, all we can say is, 'Gosh, I wonder what it was.''

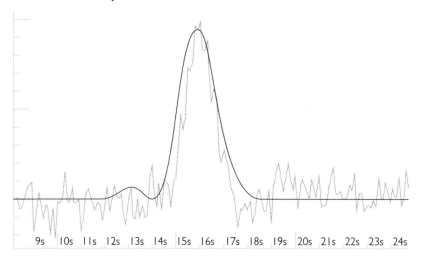

9s 10s 11s 12s 13s 14s 15s 16s 17s 18s 19s 20s 21s 22s 23s 24s

WTF STAR

The strangest of the bunch is known as **the WTF star**, demonstrating that not all astronomers are so mild-mannered that all that can say is 'yikes', 'blimey' and 'blooming heck' when they find possible evidence for alien life.

The 'official' line is that it stands for Where's the Flux? Its other name is Tabby's Star, after its lead researcher Tabitha S. Boyajian.

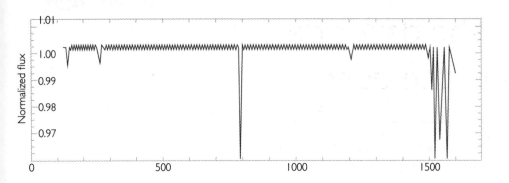

WTF, lying 1,500 light years from Earth has been the subject of much excited speculation in recent years after it was noticed that the star exhibited three weird forms of behaviour. Firstly it flickers erratically. Secondly, photos of the star from 1890 to 1990 show that WTF has faded at an unprecedented rate – nearly 15 per cent over a tiny amount of time in the life of a star. Thirdly, it is prone to strange dips in brightness, once dropping by 22 per cent during a six-month period. This behaviour is so odd, it actually displays the characteristics expected of a Kardashev Type Two alien megastructure. Ok, to explain: In 1964 Soviet astronomer Nikolai Kardashev established a hypothetical scale for measuring the degree of sophistication of any civilization based on the extent to which it can harness energy from its galaxy.

Type One civilization, like our own, is able to harness energy from its own planet and store energy from its parent sun, e.g. humans. **Type Two** can harness all the energy from its parent sun; which means it really would have no problem with everyone reaching for their kettles after The Queen's Speech on Christmas Day. **Type Three** is able to harness the entire energy of its own galaxy, which means they're the kind of civilization you really wouldn't want to get in an argument with.

Could WTF really be the result of an alien power station harnessing its power? Its behaviour is so unlike anything else observed in the universe, there's something weird going on for sure. Keep watching the skies. DB

The dark side of the dune

Singing sand dunes, squeaky beaches and whistling whelks

'This desert is the abode of many evil spirits, which amuse travellers to their destruction with most extraordinary illusions. These spirits, or djinn, at times fill the air with the sounds of all kinds of musical instruments, and also of drums and the clash of arms.'

So wrote the great Italian adventurer in *The Travels of Marco Polo*, during his travels through China's Lop Desert in the 13th century. Mysterious desert sounds bewildered Darwin too, who wrote of 'bellowing dunes' in *The Voyage of the Beagle*. Both men could have been forgiven for thinking these ominous sounds were created by evil spirits; such throbbing, thunderous hums would still scare the willies out of any lone traveller, unfamiliar with this **bizarre desert phenomena**.

Singing Sand Dunes are rare. Only 30–40 are known to exist, found in the driest, most isolated areas of the world's deserts. The sound is triggered by movement: a gust of wind or scuttling lizard can be enough to set them off. Slide down one on your backside and a 'sand symphony' can be heard up to ten miles away. While some dunes sing at a particular pitch – the Sand Mountain in Nevada knocks out a good low C – others are capable of producing multiple notes simultaneously. So what do these dunes actually sound like? Imagine the low, brooding strings at the beginning of Strauss's *Also Sprach Zarathustra* crossed with a low throaty didgeridoo. Now add to the mix mid-seventies Barry White indulging in a little Mongolian throat singing and you're half way there.

Scientific study of singing sand dunes – aeolian research – has unearthed details about the conditions that appear to produce the sounds. Size of the sand granules is a key factor: they need to be

Even more curious are the magnetic Shifting Sands of Olduvai Gorge in Tanzania. This crescent-shaped volcanic ash dune moves around 10 metres per year. The black sand is magnetic due to high levels of iron; throw it into the air and, rather than blowing away, it will clump back together and be pulled back towards the dune.

medium grain and well sorted. The dunes will often only sing on days with no wind or cloud, so the drier the sand, the better. Hence the actual side of the dune that sings is the darker, steeper slip face, which is more protected from the elements. But beyond these contributing factors, how and why the sands sing remains unanswered.

Squeaky beaches are far more common and easier to find. They do not however, possess such sonic gravitas; the sound is much higher pitched and lacking in reverberation. Walking or running across one is the aural equivalent of sneakers on a parquet floor or, in the case

Sand Mountain, Nevada, USA
The dune, which sings in a low C, looms besides Highway 50, America's loneliest road according to *Life* magazine.

Porth Oer, Snowdonia, UK
These sands squeak when you walk on them in warm weather.

Kelso Dunes, California, USA
Slide down the 'booming dunes' for a low-frequency rumble.

Kauai Barking Sands, Hawaii, USA
Home to the Pacific Missile Range Facility, where the US tests missiles and launches spacecraft.

Tarfaya, Morocco
Scientists say the sand moans at 105 hertz (Hz) — that's G-sharp, two octaves below middle C.

Mar de Dunas, Atacama Desert, Copiapo Province, Chile
Slightly higher pitched than others, the Mar de Dunas knocks out an F.

SINGING SAND DUNES OF THE WORLD

of the Whistling Sands of Porthor, Wales, like the soggy chirp of a small bird. Squeaky beaches tend to be most common where the sand is at its whitest and, as with singing dunes, when the sand is dry and granules uniform and round. Squeaky beaches are, however, in decline; some have recently stopped making sounds altogether – another mystery that is yet to be solved. And what of whistling whelks you ask? Of course whelks don't whistle, that would be ridiculous. *DB*

Altyn-Emel National Park, Kazakhstan
Four enormous and unmoving dunes that give out a deep belly rumble akin to thunder.

Mingsha Shan, Dunhuang, China
Anything more than a light breeze produces gentle, dulcet sounds akin to music.

Hongory Els, Gobi Desert, Mongolia
In dry weather, these smooth, round sand particles create an eerie tone.

Mesaieed, Qatar
Known for its low-frequency hum.

Nima Sand Museum, Kotogahama Beach, Japan
A sand museum housed in six pyramids, complete with the world's largest hourglass and artwork utilizing the acoustic sands of nearby squeaky beach, Kotogahama.

Skeleton Coast Park, Namibia, Africa
These dunes roar and rumble; you can feel the sound as much as hear it.

The Residents

The world's most mysterious band

In the 1970s, Zolar X, a short-lived, mediocre glam rock band, appeared in America. They sang and spoke in a made-up language, dressed as aliens and claimed to be from another planet. Until, that is, they were discovered to be from LA, where most of the population are just as weird.

Disguise has long been used to great effect by music groups, from Daft Punk, Insane Clown Posse and Kiss to Slipknot (who, let's be honest, would have benefitted from keeping their masks on after revealing themselves to be another bunch of middle-aged guys who look like Metallica). But there comes a time, it seems, when every costumed band gets the urge to unmask and reveal their true selves to the world. Except one: The Residents.

While their giant eyeball heads are iconic, the actual identity of The Residents has remained an enigma for over 40 years. Their music, so far from the mainstream, is even now rarely heard on the radio. The band have never conducted an interview together or so much as hinted as to their true identities. Over the decades, there have been inevitable rumours as to who's underneath those giant eyeballs. George Harrison, Van Halen, Bon Jovi, David Byrne and Matt Groenig are just a few who have all been mooted at some point.

To get around the tricky issues of needing to communicate with the world at large, all information about The Residents is filtered through their 'PR' company The Cryptic Corporation – a dedicated team who some believe includes members of the band, though this remains unverified. Documentaries and books about The Residents acknowledge that much of their information is based on speculation and stories fed to them by the Cryptic Corporation. Some, like Matt Groenig's *Official W.E.I.R.D. Book of The Residents* – yes he's a huge fan – are a deliberate mix of fact, fiction and mischief. With this in mind, what follows is merely what we think we know about the world's most unknowable band.

MEET THE RESIDENTS

The Residents seemed to materialize fully formed out of the
psychedelia-drenched counter-culture of California, combining
Dadaism with experimental sounds. According to one of their
spokesmen from the Cryptic Corporation, the tape recorder was
more important to them than the guitar. Their first record, *Meet The
Residents* (1974) featured a graffitied album cover of *Meet The Beatles*
(their faces scrawled in silly doodles) and credits members as 'John
Crawfish, George Crawfish, Paul McCrawfish, and Ringo Starfish'.
It opens with 'Boots', a bizarre take on the song, 'These Boots Were
Made For Walking' with a distant voice repeating 'walk over you',
before the album slips into a lo-fi patchwork of thumping piano riffs,
nasal comic voices, tape collage, sound effects and nonsense verse.

The Residents
pose in their
latest attire.

The first appearance of those iconic eyeball heads, from the artwork for their 1979 album, *Eskimo*.

Unable to find a label brave enough to publish their music, *Meet The Residents* was released on their own label, Ralph Records, paving the way for a DIY ethos that offered artistic freedom but also years of relative obscurity. A dark primal quality haunts the first album, setting the tone for what would follow, notably the brilliant 1979 album *Eskimo*, a homage to Inuit culture, and laced with dark chants, atmospheric keyboards, tribal sounds and field recordings. The eyeball heads made their first appearance on the cover of this album too.

Eskimo took three years to make and, as a concept album, was designed for immersive listening. It is not a record to be 'dipped into'. Never a band to tread water, The Residents 1980 release *The Commercial Album* comprised of 40 one-minute tracks, inventive bursts of weirdness, which included guest vocals from Lene Lovich and Andy Partridge (XTC). As part of the promotion for the album, the songs were aired in 40 separate one-minute slots during the advertising breaks on San Francisco's popular radio station KFRC over a three-day period, blurring the lines between advertising and art.

From there, the band continued to pioneer work with video, theatre, projections and digital technology. By 2010, the eyeball masks had been retired and The Residents presented a new image to the world: a slimmed-down three-piece – Bob, Chuck and Randy – in black rubber masks, Father Christmas outfits, goggles and ridiculously long ties. Over the decades the band have sported everything from fish heads, space helmets and clown outfits to Nixon masks, yet the eyeballs remain their defining trademark, a reminder that The Residents were never just an experimental music outfit but a unique blend of sound and performance art.

For the wary traveller, The Residents back catalogue of over 60 albums can seem like an impenetrable jungle. The music is challenging, sometimes for being too wilfully avant-garde, other times for not being more so. For some, their music can come across as arch and soulless, while the growly affected vocals of Randy – especially on later albums – can grate very quickly. But for the determined seeker, great riches can be found, with *Eskimo* and *The Commercial Album* being good entry points. At their best, The Residents are a peerless innovative wonderland of dark, primal Dadaism. Their influence can be heard and seen in Devo, They Might Be Giants, Talking Heads, KLF and The Tiger Lillies, to name but a few.

THE EYES HAVE IT

It has long been noted that the 'caveman' or 'cavewoman' never signed their art. Increasingly, in our celebrity obsessed culture, the signature *is* the art. We obsess over our rock stars and actors, keen to know their every whim, interest and eating habits. To resist such flattery and attention can't be easy, especially if, in the case of The Residents, you'd upheld 40 years of silence. Having named their alter-egos in 2010, lead singer Randy took to announcing: 'Hey everybody, it's me, Randy, singer for the Residents!' when on stage. While still anonymous, owing to a rubber head-mask and mad professor hair, Rose *has* conducted interviews about his role as frontman. How much is fact and fiction remains open to speculation, including whether Rose has been with the band since its inception or is a relatively recent addition. Despite this, the question 'Who are the Residents?' remains unanswered. In 2012, *The Residents Ultimate Box Set* became a permanent exhibit at New York's MOMA. It took the form of a fridge, containing their entire back catalogue, topped off with an original eyeball mask. No band members were present to give a speech for its unveiling. The Residents continue to let their weirdness speak for itself. DB

123

SEEKERS' DIRECTORY

Ghost radio

RADIO In Britain it is still a crime to listen to unregistered stations or to tell anyone what you hear. If you're willing to take the risk, have a fiddle with your shortwave radio or go to bit.ly/MysteriumShortWave to browse a free, high-quality shortwave radio built by a Dutch University. Trawl the populated sections between 1.6 and 30MHz and see what you can decipher.

AUDIO Akin Fernandez archived hundreds of recordings from numbers stations and noise stations and released a five-CD set of entitled *The Conet Project* (1997): soundcloud.com/the-conet-project

MUSIC The Conet Project has achieved cult status and counts many musicians among its fans. You can hear these ephemeral transmissions in the music of Boards of Canada, Stereolab, Wilco (Yankee Hotel Foxtrot) and Oddfellow's Casino (*The Water Between Us*).

PODCAST *Welcome to Nightvale* is a twice-monthly podcast in the style of community updates for the small desert town of Night Vale. WZZZ is the local numbers station, broadcast from a tall antenna at the back of an abandoned gas station on Oxford Street. A monotone female voice reads random numbers, interspersed with chimes, every hour and every day: welcometonightvale.com

The Hum

DOCUMENTARY *Punt PI: The Hum* (2016). In this episode of his Radio 4 series, comedian Stephen Punt attempts to get the bottom of The Hum.

TELEVISION *The X-Files: Drive* (1998). Mulder and Scully investigate the bizarre case of the Crumps, a couple who feel the effects of a US Navy antenna emitting ELF waves directly beneath their property. OK, maybe don't watch this if you're actually suffering from a case of the 'hums'.

JOIN A SUPPORT GROUP Share your experiences with other sufferers at facebook.com/lowfrequencyhumsufferers/ Or call the Low Frequency Noise Sufferers Helpline on (44)2380 268 741.

DOWNLOAD THE APP Spectrum analyser is a handy app that shows, in real time, the frequencies you can hear around you and those that you can't.

The Portsmouth Sinfonia

MUSIC *Portsmouth Sinfonia Plays The Popular Classics* (1974). Unarguably their finest hour: 'Also Sprach Zarathustra' will have you rolling on the floor in tears of

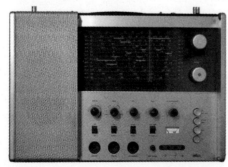

laughter in less than a minute. '5/5 for humour 1/5 for musicianship' says one Amazon reviewer.

ACTIVITY Form your own scratch orchestra and hire the Albert Hall. If you do, let us know; we'd love to come.

Space oddities

AUDIO Taking its title from a collection of Herman Hesse stories, 'Strange News from Another Star', is also a song from the album *Blur* (1997) by Blur. 'All I want to be is washed out by the sea / No death star over me / Won't give me any peace / All I want is light relief.' We didn't say it was uplifting listening, but it is a good tune.

FIELD TRIP Perkin's Observatory, Ohio. The radio telescope known as Big Ear was built and operated here between 1963 to 1998; it was famous in part for its work on SETI and the WOW! Signal detected in 1977.

The dark side of the dune

BOOK *Dune*, Frank Herbert (1965). The seed for this epic sci-fi was sown for Herbert when he travelled to Florence, Oregon, and witnessed dunes that could 'swallow whole cities, lakes, rivers, highways'.

The Residents

MUSIC *Meet The Residents* (1974) is the band's debut album. The first iteration featured a parody on the *Meet the Beatles* cover artwork, which angered the record company who threatened to sue. The second iteration reigned things somewhat by portraying 'John Crawfish, George Crawfish, Paul McCrawfish and Ringo Starfish' as sea creatures wearing Beatles suits.

Eskimo (1979) is best listened to with eyes closed, headphones on and a spare blanket to hand. Whatever the weather, it will chill you to the bone.

FILM In 1972, The Residents began a film called *Vileness Fats*. The plot revolved around a village under siege by bandits who steal their meat supply forcing the villagers to live on vegetables. To set matters straight, the locals hire Siamese twin tag-team wrestlers. The film was (sadly) never completed; *Whatever Happened to Vileness Fats?* (1985) spins together 32 minutes of footage, which hints at what would have been one of the oddest films in history.

supernature

Freaque waves

Monstrous things happen at sea

Measuring the length of two and a half football pitches, and the pride of the German merchant navy, the super-tanker MS *München* was said to be 'unsinkable'. If Leonardo DiCaprio films have taught us anything over the years, it's that making bold statements like this is a recipe for a wet dinner.

In December 1978, bound for Savannah, Georgia, the *München* ploughed into a North Atlantic storm that had been raging since November that year. It wasn't a great cause for concern; this was her 62nd voyage and she was made for conditions such as these. Unfortunately, what the ship wasn't prepared for was a phenomenon that scientists, at this point, agreed was impossible.

Between 3.10am and 3.20am on 13 December, nearby freighters received fragments of SOS calls in Morse code. One translated as '50 degrees starboard', suggesting that the ship was listing in heavy seas. Further calls transmitted until 4.43am, then ceased. The following day, a Belgian amateur radio enthusiast picked up a weak Mayday message on a frequency normally used by a German radio station. The Dutch salvage tug *Smit Rotterdam* was sent to the ship's last known position, where it eventually coordinated over 100 other vessels and 16 aircraft in maritime's largest attempted ocean rescue. After days of combing the area, all that could be found was four battered lifeboats and a scattering of buoys and life vests.

There was only one clue to the disappearance of the world's safest ship: a pummelled starboard lifeboat, which would ordinarily have hung off the ship 20 metres above the waterline. The steel pins that attached the boat to the *München* had been bent backwards, suggesting a tremendous force had torn the craft from the vessel. Disregarding an attack from a giant sea beast, all evidence pointed towards a rogue wave. The court investigation concluded that 'an unusual event' sank the *München*. Mariners, however, knew the true story.

Ever since seafarers have kept ships' logs, there have been **tales of unexpected, monstrous waves**. Columbus encountered one of these

Merchant ships and freighters are built to withstand rough seas, but not waves three times the size expected.

A merchant ship labours through heavy seas as a huge wave looms ahead, Bay of Biscay, 1940.

'unusual events' during his third voyage in 1498. On the southern tip of Trinidad, a wave higher than the ship's mast hoisted his entire fleet up on to its crest, dropping them into a deep trough and leading him to name the channel Mouth of the Serpent. In 1853, sailing from Liverpool to Canada, the emigrant-carrying vessel Annie Jane was struck by a freak wave off the coast of Barra in the Hebrides; the poop deck collapsed, crushing 200 people to death. Only four years before the *München*'s disappearance, Norwegian tanker *Wilstar* had her bow clean ripped off.

LOST AT SEA

It's the best-kept secret of the shipping industry: **every week, two freighters are lost**. Some succumb to pirates; others are bombed for 'acting suspiciously'; cargos of cement shift in their holds and tip them up; fatigued crews run their vessels aground. The ocean is still the world's most dangerous place to work, with 2000 seafarers losing their lives per year. It's not something we think about. Losses are often only reported in trade press. Ports are far removed from towns and most seafarers are Filipino, Polish, Romanian; it's not something that stirs the British media. We're too busy reporting on missing passenger planes anyway. The circumstances surounding many of these lost ships remains unexplained – perhaps down to the fact that oceanographers have only begun to investigate one particular cause in the past two decades.

This figure accounts for freighters, tankers and large commercial ships; it doesn't include smaller vessels and fishing craft.

11 March 1943: an enormous wave breaks over the island of Rockall in the North Atlantic Ocean. The wave's height over the west side is estimated to be 170 feet and was captured by an RAF Coastal Command aircraft during World War II.

Freaque waves – a recently formed (and rather unnecessary) portmanteau of 'freak' and 'rogue' – recognizes the unexpected occurrence of unpredictable, monster waves that arise in our open oceans. They can take out the world's largest ocean liners, leaving no time to put out a Mayday call. One minute there's a ship ploughing its way through rough seas, the next there's a scattering of lifebuoys on the surface.

Rare, unforeseeable and exceedingly dangerous, freaque waves – we're going to stop using that word now, it's silly – rogue waves are defined by oceanographers as waves that **more than double the significant wave height**. Rogues are distinct from tsunamis, which are caused by landslides or the displacement of water following a sudden movement on the ocean floor. While terrifying and destructive, tsunamis are at least explainable and (to some extent) **predictable**.

At the time of the *München* investigation, however, the existence of rogue waves was deemed impossible. Despite countless anecdotal claims, reports were widely discredited as myths of the sea – the mariner's version of 'the fish that got away'. Then, of course, there was the fact that many of those who've observed the phenomena didn't live to tell the tale.

At this point, wave behaviour was predicted using what's known as the linear model, which establishes the limit for how big the largest wave will be in any given sea state. BBC's *Horizon* episode 'Freak Wave' (2002) plunges into the subject in frightening detail, with footage that would give even Captain Ahab a dicky tummy.

THE WAVES THAT SIMPLY SHOULDN'T EXIST

Dr Jim Gunson of the Met Office points to a bell-shaped graph and explains why, according to the linear model, rogue waves are simply impossible: '[the graph] gives the probability of a certain wave height. It's like the population of children in a class. There is an average height of children – and most children are around that height. Some are quite a bit taller or shorter, but the chance that a child is three or four times the height of the average child is very, very small.' ('Freak Wave', Horizon, BBC, 2002).

Using this model – which the shipping industry relies on to calculate ship stretch and to design freighters – even in storms with 12-metre waves, the chances of being struck by a 30-metre behemoth is practically zero.

Everything changed in 1995. A rogue wave – the Draupner Wave (or New Year's Wave) – was finally detected, in the North Sea, using scientific equipment. It was a monster: a tremendous 25.6-metre beast in a sea of 12-metre ripples. That's the height of an eight-story building.

Five years later, in 2000, British oceanographic vessel RRS *Discovery* recorded a 29-metre wave near Rockall, off the coast of Scotland – at the time, the largest ever measured by scientific instruments. Analysis concluded that 'none of the state-of-the-art weather forecasts and wave models – the information upon which all

The significant wave height is defined as the mean wave height (trough to crest) of the highest third of the waves measured.

The more cautious can even follow Twitter alerts from the National Tsunami Warning Centre (@NWS_NTWC), which charts seismic activity and generates event image showing waves radiating from earthquakes, with travel times.

ships, oil rigs, fisheries, and passenger boats rely – had predicted these behemoths'. According to all the theoretical methods at the time, these waves should simply not have existed.

Further investigation revealed that not only were these rogues tall, they were also steeper than normal waves, and they were occurring with alarming frequency. Research focused for a time on South Africa, where ships are regularly mangled by the sea: returning to shore with double-decker bus sized bites out of their sides, with bows ripped right off, or sliced in two on their maiden voyages.

Plotting the locations of damaged or sunken ships over an infra-red map of the Agulhas current, it was believed that these oceanic beasts reared up when storms travelling northwards met with warm water moving down the coast. The mystery appeared solved – until something happened in the South Atlantic that shattered all explanations.

In February 2001, the MS *Caledonian Star* was returning from a cruise around the Antarctic, carrying 105 British and American tourists in their autumn years who were about to wish they'd booked a narrowboat holiday. The ship was as strong as they come, built to cut

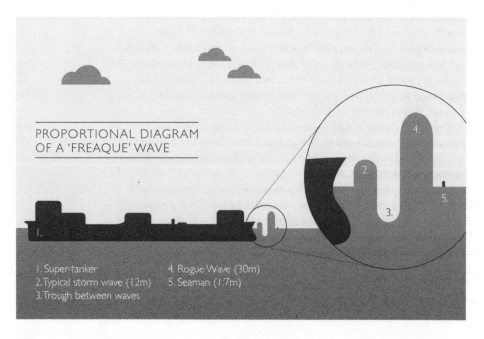

PROPORTIONAL DIAGRAM
OF A 'FREAQUE' WAVE

1. Super-tanker
2. Typical storm wave (12m)
3. Trough between waves
4. Rogue Wave (30m)
5. Seaman (1.7m)

A merchant ship labours through heavy seas as a huge wave looms ahead, Bay of Biscay, 1940.

through ice and weather rough seas, so the bad weather report didn't worry the crew. She rode the 12-metre waves with ease.

But then, First Officer Goran Persson spotted something on the horizon. A mile away, approaching fast, was a wave twice the height of all others – a 30-metre, sheer wall of water. Free-falling into the trough, all aboard fell against the walls, as the wave collapsed upon the ship and exploded into the bridge, leaving Goran to swim back to the controls through freezing water. Then, as soon as it appeared, it was gone, leaving the Caledonian Star without radar or sonar, but fortunately still with a working engine.

THEORY FIT FOR A MONSTER

With no warm currents to explain the wave, it was time for a new theory. It came, unexpectedly, from a completely different branch of science: the non-linear world of quantum physics. Al Osborne from the University of Turin argued that a modified version of the Schrödinger equation held the answer: 'The equation describes a theoretical water surface where huge waves can suddenly leap up out of nowhere, where for some reason normal waves become unstable and grow huge.' ('Freak Wave', *Horizon*, BBC, 2002).

He describes a scenario where monster waves steal energy from their neighbours, generating one uber-wave surrounded by two smaller, and a deep trough on either side. Not only were these freak waves enormous, they were a different shape: vertical walls of solid water, which had the capacity to break, even way out at sea. These waves really were going rogue.

The theory described exactly what the MS *Caledonian Star* had experienced – and was identical to graphs of the Draupner Wave in 1995. Quantum physics had unearthed what had been sinking ships for centuries.

Mystery solved? Pretty much, but we're still left with a sobering thought: no ships are currently built to withstand the force exerted by a rogue wave. Seagoing vessels are designed to cope with undulating waves up to a certain height. A freak 30-metre wave deploys a force of 100 tons per square metre. The strongest ships can withhold 15 tons without damage (30 tons if they dent); a 100-ton impact could rip a ship in two.

Satellite imagery and radar data now regularly observes waves with a crest-to-trough height of 20 to 30 metres, many times a day throughout the world's oceans. Just to keep things interesting, Australian scientists have also proven the existence of 'rogue wave holes', inverted freak waves. There's even been talk of 'super-rogue waves', which measure up to five times the average sea state.

Investigators now agree that the MS *München* was most likely struck by a freakish wall of water in the dead of night. Falling into the trough, the wave would have then broken over her, ripping away the lifeboats, smashing through the windows of the bridge and flooding the engine. Listing without power or steering, it wasn't long before the ocean claimed her. When your nearest land is two miles below, there's little hope of survival. JK

Ball lightning

Singed soil or the key to spontaneous
human combustion?

A 2.4-metre raging ball of fire enters a church, smashing pews,
filling the nave with a sulphurous odour and killing four parishioners
outright. A globe of light descends slowly from the sky to roll
harmlessly around a farmyard until it's sniffed by a pig and explodes.
A ball appears inside the cabin of a plane and floats down the aisle.
A fiery blob bounces on a Russian's teacher's head 20 times before
vanishing. A luminous basketball ricochets into the basement of a
house, wrecking an old mangle. ('Ball lightning scientists remain in
the dark', *New Scientist*, 2001).

People have witnessed ball lightning – glowing spheres of electricity
that can drift through walls, 'attack' ships and crack pavements – for
centuries. Photos shared online show blazing speech bubbles of
electricity, said to hover above the ground for up to a minute. Some
have even suggested the phenomenon could account for cases of

18 Sept, 2014:
ball lightning
hovers over Wells
Road in Bristol, UK.

To my illustrious friend Sir William Crookes
of whom I always think and whose kind
letters I never answer!
Nikola Tesla

In 1752, deciding that it wasn't going to be feasible to get his 30-foot lightning rod high enough into the sky, Benjamin Franklin performed an experiment where he flew a kite in a storm, attempting to collect the electrical charge in a Leyden Jar.

spontaneous human combustion. Two hundred and sixty-five years after Benjamin Franklin performed the first systematic study of lightning – **by flying a kite in a thunderstorm, the nutter** – scientists and mystery seekers alike are still clearly baffled by this atmospheric monster.

Until the 1960s, scientists treated the idea of ball lightning with scepticism. Most of the evidence for its existence was anecdotal and accounts differed wildly: it was harmless and lethal; it was transparent, translucent, radiating flames and shaped like a disk; it passed through solid metal and wood without effect and burned everything it touched; it violently exploded, dissipated and vanished with a benign 'pop'.

What we had here was a shape-shifting and undefinable phenomena, which is always going to give scientists sweaty palms. In 1972, Dr Neil Charman, lecturer at the University of Manchester, attempted to rationalize the anecdotes. Writing a paper in the *New Scientist*, he discouraged seeking answers in these visual observations: 'Many of the reports have a certain mediaeval aura of witchcraft and magic about them, which scarcely serves to endear them to the sceptics,' he wrote. ('The enigma of ball lightning', *New Scientist*,

1972). However, reading through thousands of eyewitness accounts dating back to the 17th century and including notes from Tsar Nicholls II and Aleister Crowley, Charman picked out a number of common characteristics exhibited by a '**typical lightning ball**'. These included: appearing simultaneously with a cloud-to-ground lightning strike; being spherical or pear-shaped with fuzzy edges; exuding an odour of sulphur, ozone or nitrogen oxide; being as bright as a table lamp; moving horizontally or wandering erratically.

Ball lightning is distinct from St Elmo's Fire: a bright blue or violet glow emitting from tall, pointy structures -- ship masts, church spires, aircraft antennae, even the tips of cattle horns.

THE KEY TO SPONTANEOUS HUMAN COMBUSTION?

Since then, several theories have emerged, some using experiments that feel as maverick as Franklin's kite flying antics. The most well-received came from John Abrahamson, a now-retired chemical engineer from the University of Canterbury in New Zealand, who in 2000 proposed that lightning could vaporize silicate particles in soil, producing globes of slow burning silicon. Blown into the air, the silicon vapour condensed and spontaneously formed a 'globular network of long chains'. ('Spontaneous combustion', *New Scientist*, 2000). Together with colleague James Dinniss, the pair performed their own **Tesla-esque experiments**, generating miniature silicon chains of electricity in the lab but not a fully-fledged ball.

Incidentally, Nikola Tesla was a dab hand at producing ball lightning; he could make 38-cm spheres but, being more interested in the really powerful stuff, made them more out of curiosity.

Since then, scientists in both Tel Aviv and China have successfully managed to produce actual balls of flame by firing mock lightning at sheets of silicon oxide. It sounds like science is getting there, but results remain inconclusive.

As for spontaneous human combustion? For that, we need to leave the comfort of scientific study and venture back into anecdote. In 1989, a 27-year-old engineer stopped for a tinkle by the roadside, near Budapest. His wife, who remained in the car, saw the young man surrounded by a strange blue light: 'He opened his arms wide and fell to the ground. His wife ran to him, noticing that one of his tennis shoes had been torn off. Although it looked hopeless she tried to help him, and soon after she was able to stop a passing bus. Amazingly, the bus was filled with medical doctors returning from a meeting; unhappily they immediately pronounced the man was dead.' ('Spontaneous Combustion', *Journal of Meteorology*, 1990).

An autopsy revealed that the poor chap's lungs were damaged and his stomach had been carbonized, suggesting 'human combustion'. However, the blue light and blown off trainer pointed to an atmospheric event. If nothing else it's a stark reminder to always check the skies before hopping out of the car for a quick Jimmy Riddle. JK

137

Atmospheric lightning

Here come the blue jets

Witness a thunderstorm from a plane and you might, with growing trepidation, notice how lightning doesn't just strike the ground. It can also ripple between clouds and streak upwards, dissipating high into the atmosphere. It's a phenomenon that has long been reported by pilots, but was brushed off by meteorologists until the first recorded observation of a 'blue jet' by the Space Shuttle in 1989. This was quickly followed by the first colour image of a 'sprite' in 1994 and a recording of ELVES in 1990. Sprites and elves appearing around aeroplanes? Don't worry, we're not about to prove the existence of **gremlins** akin to the fellow who gives Shatner the shits in *The Twilight Zone*. Known as transient luminous events, these very real (but still not thoroughly explained) phenomena are happening high in the sky above you right now.

'Nightmare at 20,000 Feet' is episode 123 of *The Twilight Zone*, which originally aired on 11 October, 1963. William Shatner plays Mr. Robert Wilson, a 37-year-old salesman recovering from a nervous breakdown who sees something rather unsettling out of the plane window. Watch it at your peril.

RED SPRITES

Up where the air is clear, lightning isn't white or steely blue, it's red, orange and green. It can cover huge areas of the upper atmosphere, even tickling the border with space. The most common of these transient luminous events are known as sprites – large-scale electrical discharges that occur in the mesosphere high above cumulonimbus clouds, triggered by discharges of cloud-to-ground lightning. Named after Shakespeare's Puck and Ariel, these red-orange flashes, occurring 25–55 miles above the ground and lasting only a fraction of a second, have a halo and long dangling tendrils, look for all the world like a giant sky jellyfish.

BLUE JETS

Closer to the ground, blue jets are narrow cones of energy that discharge from the top of a cumulonimbus cloud upwards into the lowest levels of the ionosphere, 25–30 miles above the Earth. Unlike sprites, they're not always triggered by lightning, but possibly from hail within thunderstorms. The phenomena was first recorded in 1989 on a monochrome video of a storm taken by the Space Shuttle

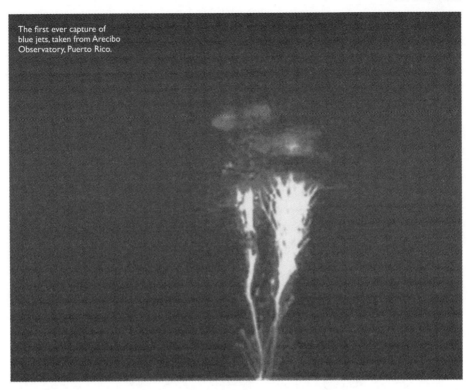

The first ever capture of blue jets, taken from Arecibo Observatory, Puerto Rico.

as it passed over Australia. Since then, 'gigantic jets' have also been observed above a thunderstorm in the South China Sea: double the height of blue jets, the five discharges recorded in 2002 reached 35–34 miles into the atmosphere, their shapes likened to trees and carrots.

ELVES

Clearly delighted with the fairy analogy, meteorologists coined the acronym ELVES – or Emission of Light and Very Low Frequency perturbations due to Electromagnetic Pulse Sources. These 250-mile-diameter, donut-shaped pulses of red light occur in the ionosphere, 62 miles above a thunderstorm. ELVES are even trickier, as they're the briefest of transient luminous events, lasting less than a thousandth of a second. In 1996, researchers from Stanford University, California, built a super sensitive instrument called the 'Fly's Eye' to look at different portions of the sky. Following storms in Colorado, they discovered that ELVES formed 150 microseconds after a lightning strike, often followed by a second, dimmer, 'elf'.

Red Sprites at Paranal Observatory in Chile from the VLT platform by Petr Horálek /ESO. Enlargement below.

This sprite lightning lasted a fraction of a second and was likely more than 500km away at a height of 80km.

DARK LIGHTNING

NASA's Fermi Gamma-ray Space Telescope was launched in 2008 to study flares powered by black holes and outbursts from supernovas. In 2011, it was hit by a beam of high-energy positrons, the anti-matter

Hafar Al Batin (Saudi Arabia)

Lightning

Khajfi
(Saudi Arabia)

Kuwait City

equivalent of electrons. Worryingly, the beam didn't come from outer space; it came from an Earthbound thunderstorm over Namibia. It appeared that the Earth's magnetic field had focused 100 trillion positrons emitted from the storm into an intense beam, which struck the satellite at almost the speed of light. Scientists speculate that it's all down to 'dark lightning' – an extreme form of lightning that generates little light but blasts out huge amounts of gamma rays. If you thought pilots must get anxious flying through storms, imagine how it must feel for astronauts, knowing that the Earth produces thousands of these terrestrial gamma-ray flashes per day. *JK*

Scientists have found evidence that terrestrial gamma-ray flashes may occur in the atmosphere as often as 500 times a day. ABOVE: An astronaut aboard the International Space Station takes a photo of lightning above Kuwait and Saudi Arabia, in 2013.

SUPER CATS

Dogs may be man's best friend, but cats are undoubtedly the internet's. Without them, the web would be an awfully quiet place. We seem to spend more of our time watching videos of cats being freaked out by cucumbers than anything else. Even Wikipedia serves up a feline 'who's who', with pages on meme cats (Cats That Look Like Hitler), celebrity felines (Grumpy Cat) and 'lolcats' which, if you've never heard of, you're better off not knowing. And while it's a genuine mystery why felines beat canines hands down in the OMG-I-must-upload-my-pet-doing-something-cute-on-to-YouTube' rating, that's not the focus of this feature. Instead, it is about cats with extraordinary abilities. Not exactly superhuman powers, but certainly superfeline.

Cat Mandu

1995–2002

The only feline to be named leader of a long-standing political group, Cat Mandu served the UK's Monster Raving Loony Party from 1999 to 2002, following the sudden death of its founder, Screaming Lord Sutch. While conceived as a joke party, the Monster Raving Loonies are still going strong in the UK, despite losing over 40 by-elections since their inception in 1982. Their policies include the protection of unicorns, the introduction of a 99p coin and 'for all secret data to be placed in a brown bag and hidden in the PM's socks and pants drawer'.

Since 1995, Cat Mandu lived with the party's deputy leader Alan 'Howling Laud' Hope, though their relationship was very much one of equals rather than Cat Mandu being simply 'Alan's moggy'.

After Sutch's death, both Hope and Cat Mandu stood for the role of party leader but – following a split vote – it was decided they would share the role, with Cat Mandu as the official face of the party, owing to the fact that he was better looking.

During his three-year reign, Cat Mandu served the Loonies well before a fatal traffic accident whisked him off to moggy heaven and left the party with little option but to make 'Howling Laud' Hope sole leader. Rumours that the black car that caused Cat Mandu's demise was driven by then UK Prime Minister Tony Blair have never been substantiated, though eyewitness accounts of a driver with power-crazed eyes do lend credence to the theory.

Cat Burglar

2006-present

Dusty is a ten-year-old cat who lives in San Mateo, California, with his owner Jean Chu and is unique among felines for being excessively light-fingered. Or perhaps should that be light-pawed? Over the years he has stolen close to a thousand items from local households, including bras, blankets, shoes (correctly paired), bikinis, kids' toys, towels, balls, dog collar, frisbee and gloves. The thieving normally takes place at night when the items are retrieved from neighbouring houses and dragged back into Dusty's home. By 2011, Klepto Kitty (as he became known) had become something of a celebrity in the US, even making a guest appearance on *Late Show With David Letterman.*

While Dusty's thieving has diminished in recent years, this is largely down to his neighbours getting wise to his antics and being more careful about what they leave around their houses. Of course Dusty has his own Facebook page. As well as featuring correspondence with global fans, it also contains regular updates and photos of stolen items uploaded by his owner. This way at least it gives his neighbours' a sporting chance to be able to identify and retrieve their precious belongings.

Death Cat

2005-present

Oscar is not what you'd call a sociable cat. He has a tendency to mooch around, hisses when grumpy and is best not picked up unless you've a handy pair of gauntlets. Shortly after being adopted in 2005 by the Steere Nursing Home in Rhode Island for residents in the latter stages of dementia, however, Oscar began to demonstrate his extraordinary gift. He has an uncanny habit of knowing when a patient is facing their final hours, and will seek actively them out. If the dying patient is in a room with a locked door, Oscar will scratch until let in. He is always gentle with the dying, sleeping by them or curling up in their laps. After correctly predicting over 100 deaths in the home, Oscar become the subject of a book, *Making Rounds with Oscar,* in which author David Dosa tried to understand whether the cat is drawn to the sweet smell of the biochemical ketone – said to emanate from the dying – or if Oscar simply does have a special power. Despite rabbits, parakeets, dogs and other cats sharing Steere Nursing Home with Oscar, he is the only one drawn to those facing impending death. If it is the smell that draws him, it remains a unique behaviour for any animal.

Such is Oscar's reliability that family and friends of those living at Steere can find solace in the knowledge that when the hours are drawing near to saying farewell to their loved ones, the staff at the home will be able to let them know. Thanks to the antics of a grumpy cat. DB

The Carrington Event

When the aurora borealis goes bad

Between 28 August and 2 September 1859, a great number of sunspots began to appear on the surface of our star. English astronomer Richard C. Carrington observed the flare through the telescope at his private observatory, leading what happened next to be named the Carrington Event.

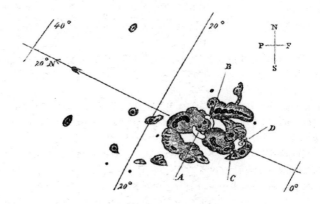

1 September 1859: English astronomer Richard Carrington drew the sunspots he observed, shortly before a solar coronal mass ejection hit the Earth.

A little over 17 hours later, a solar coronal mass ejection hit Earth's magnetosphere and induced one of the largest geomagnetic storms on record. Aurora borealis were seen as far south as Cuba and Honolulu; the glow of the northern lights over the Rocky Mountains woke gold miners, who started to make breakfast in the middle of the night; people woken in northeastern USA read newspapers as if it were daylight.

All of this seems rather strange behaviour – we'd probably be freaking out rather than putting the kettle on – but it must have been a beautiful spectacle to behold. *The Baltimore American and Commercial Advertiser* reported on the second night of the event: 'at times the light was, if possible, more brilliant, and the prismatic hues more varied and

Aurora borealis, as photographed by one of the Expedition 40 crew members aboard the International Space Station from an altitude of 223 nautical miles (2014).

An astronaut aboard the International Space Station captures the aurora spanning thousands of kilometres over Quebec, Canada (2012).

gorgeous. The light was greater than that of the moon at its fullest, but had an indescribable softness and delicacy that seemed to envelop everything upon which it rested.' (*Baltimore American and Commercial Advertiser*, 3 September 1859).

Meanwhile, as America was preparing another midnight breakfast, the technology of the time was breaking down. Telegraph systems failed, emitting electrical shocks and setting papers on fire; pylons threw sparks; telephone operators were able to send and receive messages despite having disconnected the power supply. The Victorian 'internet' was plunged into chaos.

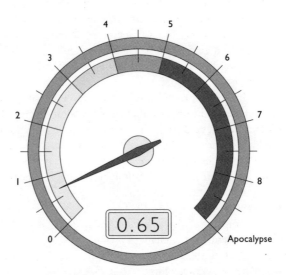

The Kp index measures the magnitude of geomagnetic storms.

AS IF WE DIDN'T HAVE ENOUGH TO WORRY ABOUT
As anyone who's sought out the aurora will know, the Kp index records the scale of global geomagnetic activity with a reading between zero and nine. It allows us to predict how the Northern Lights will behave up to an hour in advance: zero to three isn't worth getting out of bed for; four to five would be worthy of an Instagram post; six to seven would leave you speechless. But what happens when the scales reach nine? What if a Carrington-level event were to happen today? Would it bring our technology-powered world to its knees: internet servers melting, traffic lights cycling through red-to-green as if possessed, texts being sent all of their own accord, sat-navs taking you in completely the wrong direction?

In 2012, we very nearly found out. While less severe solar storms occurred in 1921 and 1960, on 23 July 2012, a coronal mass ejection on the scale of the Carrington Event tore through the Earth's orbit. Thankfully, the Earth was on the other side of its orbit. Just one week later, we would have been toast. 'If it had hit [Earth], we would still be picking up the pieces,' said Daniel Baker of the University of Colorado. ('Near Miss: The Solar Superstorm of July 2012', NASA *Science Beta*, 2014).

According to the NASA report, the process begins with a solar flare – an explosion in the magnetic canopy of a sunspot. Next, x-rays and UV radiation reach Earth, ionizing the upper layers of our atmosphere. Minutes to hours later, the energetic particles arrive, spacewalking astronauts beat a hasty retreat as electrons and protons electrify satellites. Finally, come the coronal mass ejections, billion-ton clouds of magnetized plasma that fall down upon the Earth.

By this point, not only would wall sockets stop working, power surges would blow transformers and GPS equipment – ubiquitous in mobiles, aeroplanes and cars – would be disrupted or destroyed. With satellites knocked out, card payments wouldn't go through, knocking out our banking systems. Cities would be without power for months. According to a study by the National Academy of Sciences, the economic impact could exceed $2 trillion and it would take us four to ten years to recover. The cost of replacing the satellites alone would cost between $30 and $70 billion. ('Severe Space Weather – Social and Economic Impacts', NASA *Science Beta*, 2009).

According to scientists, the chance of a solar storm the level of the 1859 event hitting the Earth in the next ten years is 12 per cent. ('Near Miss: The Solar Superstorm of July 2012', NASA *Science Beta*, 2014). Time perhaps, to start stockpiling candles and family size tins of beans, keeping bank notes under the bed and digging a latrine in the back garden. JK

ANIMAL SUICIDES:
FACT OR FICTION?

'A kind of compulsion seizes each tiny rodent and, carried along by an unreasoning hysteria, each falls into step for a march that will take them to a strange destiny. That destiny is to jump into the ocean. They've become victims of an obsession – a one-track thought: 'Move on! Move on!' This is the last chance to turn back, yet over they go, casting themselves out bodily into space … and so is acted out the legend of mass suicide.' Narration from *White Wilderness* (1958)

In Walt Disney's Oscar award-winning documentary *White Wilderness* (1958), scores of lemmings hurl themselves wantonly off a cliff edge, establishing a belief that these depressed rodents engage in acts of self-harm that many still hold to be true today. It wasn't until 1983 that Canadian Broadcasting Company documentary, *Cruel Camera*, unearthed the real truth: the scene was staged. The lemmings, flown in from Hudson Bay, couldn't be persuaded to leap from the cliff edge and so the film crew flung them into the abyss using an improvised turntable.

It was a sad day for lemmings, but thankfully the truth emerged. However, among the cruel camera tricks, and the sad but explainable whale beachings, there are tales of supposed animal 'suicide' that are still puzzling, plus one lone mammal that could really do with a hug.

The bird suicides of Jatinga, India

Every monsoon season on moonless nights, hundreds of migrating birds plunge from the sky and smash themselves to death on the streets of Jatinga, Assam. Bizarrely, the 'suicides' only occur over a thin strip of land measuring 200 m by 1.5 km, and only between the hours of 6.30pm and 9.30pm. It's been happening for the past 100 years and no one knows why. 44 species have been recorded so far, including bitterns, kingfishers, egrets and herons. If the birds are merely stunned, it's not long before they're battered to death by townsfolk, who take the aerial onslaught as a bad omen. The local government has been trying to discourage such behaviour; instead they want to cash in, set up viewing platforms and coax sadistic tourists to the town so they can watch birds inexplicably plunging to their deaths.

The Overtoun Bridge, Scotland

It's 2014 and three-year-old Cassie, a springer spaniel, is trotting across the Overtoun Bridge in West Dunbartonshire, Scotland, when – unexpectedly – she takes a leap from the balustrade and plummets 15 metres to the rocks below. Fortunately, Cassie survives but, accordingly to the tabloids, 50 other canines have not been so lucky. In Celtic Mythology, an 'overtoun' is a mysterious 'thin place' where the fabric between the spirit realm and our own is worn translucent. Could something be calling the dogs into the abyss? Or are the animals gripped by a sense of '*l'appel du vide*' – that feeling you get looking off a high vantage point and feel the urge to jump? The dogs reportedly leap from the same spot – between the final two parapets on the right-hand side – and tends to be breeds with long muzzles, such as retrievers, labradors and spaniels. The prevailing theory is that the solid granite walls, waist height on a person, block the dogs' hearing and vision. Their sense of smell in overdrive, and unaware that they're even on a bridge, the dogs get excited by the smell of mink musk below. Once they've leapt onto the wall, the momentum would be enough to carry them over the edge. A sign now warns owners to keep their dogs on a lead. Whether you believe in wafer-thin boundaries between our world and the next, or in the irresistible power of a mink's anal glands, it's advice best heeded.

The 52-hertz whale

The 'Loneliest Whale' sings at a frequency of 52 hertz; to us that would be a low bass note, but to a blue or fin whale, which sings between 10 and 40 Hz, it's positively whiney. The high-pitched call is always heard alone and some say it prevents the creature, who is thought to be a one-of-a-kind hybrid, from ever finding companionship. Marine mammal researcher Bill Watkins spent 12 years recording and analysing this particular whale's call, and he found it be utterly unique, claiming it to be one of the animal kingdom's great mysteries. Ever since the late oceanographer's research reached the press, people around the world have been touched by the notion: writing in to share their affinity with the whale that just doesn't fit in. One fellow tracked down the audio and distributes cassettes to those who find comfort in listening to the whale's call. It has even inspired a Kickstarter-funded expedition hoping to locate and film the whale (softie Leo DiCaprio put in a round $50,000 to help make it happen), as well as Kathryn Roberts' folk song 52-hertz. Unfortunately it's not been heard since 2014. Did the loneliness just get too much for the poor creature? JK

The South Atlantic Anomaly

Thomas Lynch Jnr was a man who embodied the phrase: 'and it was all going so well ...' Born in South Carolina in 1749, life started out rather nicely for the young Lynch. He studied law at Britain's renowned Middle Temple, married his childhood sweetheart and returned to South Carolina in 1772 to begin an illustrious career in politics. It's safe to say, things were peachy.

Events took a turn for the worse, however, in 1775, when Lynch was commissioned as a commander in the 1st South Carolina regiment and contracted malaria. Unable to fulfil his duties, he returned home to find his father had suffered a stroke. Aged 27, Lynch took his father's seat in Congress but, nursing a malingering fever, he eventually decided to seek out therapeutic help in France. In 1779, he set sail for Europe via the West Indies. This was the last anyone ever saw of Lynch; he and his wife, together with the entire crew, became the first recorded victims of the Bermuda Triangle.

Since then, the Bermuda Triangle – a shape defined by apexes in Florida, Bermuda and Puerto Rico – has been blamed for countless such disappearances: from the vanishing of the USS *Cyclops*, the US Navy's single largest loss of life in the history unrelated to combat, to the discovery of ghost ships and aircraft that simply fade out of radar contact, never to be seen again. Believers cite UFO encounters, the paranormal or a temporary suspension of the laws of physics as causes for the peculiar events.

The Bermuda Triangle is one of 12 such places of abject spookiness and mass disappearances. Ivan T. Sanderson, a Scottish naturalist, paranormal investigator and founder of the Society for the Investigation of the Unexplained, plotted 12 'vortices' over a map of the world in the 1960s. He focused his research on ten areas where unexplained incidents (missing ships and aircraft) or

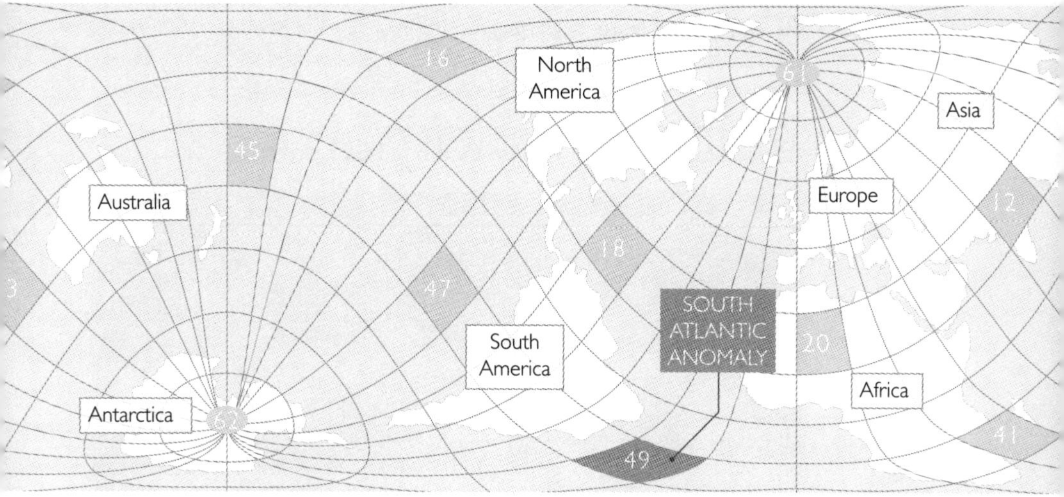
North America
Asia
Australia
Europe
South America
SOUTH ATLANTIC ANOMALY
Africa
Antarctica
16
61
45
12
18
47
20
62
49
41

The South Atlantic Anomaly is one of 12 purported 'vile vortices' arranged in a pattern around the Earth. The term was coined by Ivan T. Sanderson, who catalogued them as the sites of mysterious phenomena.

magnetic distortions had been reported. It turned out that they were approximately equidistant – five in the Tropic of Cancer, five in Capricorn – and looked rather neat on the map. He then added the two poles, perhaps to balance things out.

Sanderson speculated that air and sea currents created the electromagnetic anomalies responsible for vanishing vessels and instrument malfunctions. In 1973, Soviet scientists Nikolai Goncharov, Vyacheslav Morochov and Valery Makarov expanded on the idea in their article 'Is the Earth a Large Crystal?' published in a Soviet science magazine. They explained that 'a matrix of cosmic energy' covered the Earth with 12 pentagonal plates. At the junctions between these plates, interesting things happened: advanced prehistoric cultures, wildlife migrations, gravitational anomalies and mysterious phenomena.

Nowadays, these vortices – the Bermuda Triangle included – are generally understood to be no more significant in terms of disappearances than any other part of the ocean, home to their fair share of **extreme meteorological events and human error**. But there is one of Sanderson's vortices that still leaves NASA scientists with furrowed brows: the South Atlantic Anomaly.

In 1953, the loss of the *Kaiyo-Maru* No 5 and its crew is often attributed to the curse of the Devil's Sea. The reality was somewhat of a scientific tragedy, as the crew were investigating a very active submarine volcano called Myōjin-Shō they were simply in the wrong place at the wrong time.

CAPTAIN, SHIELDS ARE DOWN!

The Van Allen belt is a two-banded radiation field that wraps around the Earth like a lifesaver, shielding our planet from radioactive particles, such as solar flares and strong solar winds from our own sun.

The outer band traps electrons, the inner grabs the protons. This latter band circles 750–800 miles above the Earth's surface, except for at one point – just above the southern coast of Brazil – where it dips to within 120 miles of the ground.

Spacecraft usually fly well below the proton belt, but this low spot

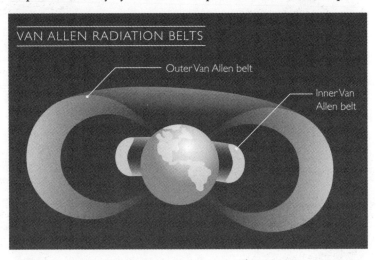

VAN ALLEN RADIATION BELTS

Outer Van Allen belt

Inner Van Allen belt

There is even evidence to suggest that the anomaly is moving and growing in strength, pointing towards the planet possibly gearing up for a magnetic shift.

places an area of **intense radiation** right in the path of our satellites, shuttles and the International Space Station (ISS). The peculiar effects of the South Atlantic Anomaly (SAA) are well documented by NASA. The Geiger counter on board America's first satellite, Explorer 1, stopped functioning when it became overloaded with radiation as far back as 1958. Computers and instruments malfunction or cease up entirely. The Hubble Space Telescope is programmed to switch off its electronics when it passes through.

To explore the effect that radiation might be having on astronauts, including within the South Atlantic Anomaly, NASA invented Radioactive Fred – a spooky-looking 3-foot tall 'Phantom Torso' that you wouldn't want to be trapped in space with – and sent him on a four-month mission on board the ISS in 2001 ('The Phantom Torso', NASA *Science Beta*, 2001). Fred, who doesn't have limbs, but does have real human bones as well as a heart, brain, thyroid and colon made from a bespoke plastic that closely matched human tissue, was fitted with 416 lithium-based (radiation detectors). Results from the experiment help predict how much radiation a human body can tolerate, informs engineers about the strength of shielding needed to

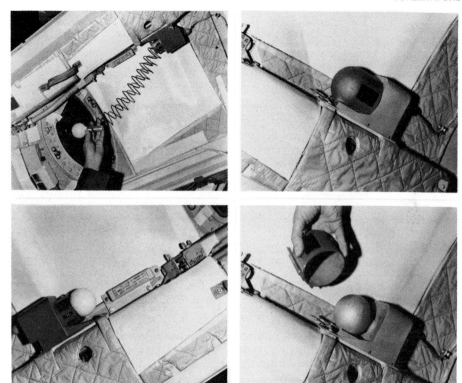

keep people safe in space and offers some guidance on what to turn off when spacecraft pass through the Anomaly. It seems that scientists are seeing it as something to learn to live with.

Beyond radiation, astronauts have also reported seeing strange lights and shooting stars when passing through the area ('Flashes seen by astronauts remain mysterious', *New Scientist*, 2003). But not normal shooting stars: phosphenes – flashes, streaks and clouds of light, with their eyes closed, believed to be particles striking sensitive areas of the retina. This is not necessarily cause for speculating that an inter-dimensional pathway exists above Brazil. It denotes something far more exciting: the SAA might be one of the places that we can see elementary particles at play. This strange anomalous space might just be a prime spot for observing some of the universe's fundamental building blocks. MI

Scientists have been measuring the effect of radiation of spacecraft and astronauts since spaceflight began. ABOVE: 1965 experiment used on Gemini-6 spaceflight when passing through the South Atlantic Anomaly.

153

Most mysterious aerial phenomena now have a satisfactory explanation: secret missile launches, surveillance blimps, aircraft contrails, weird cloud formations, St Elmo's fire, military experiments. Yet, reports of strange lights or sounds from the sky persist and there are some occurrences that even NASA can't explain. Welcome to the eerie world of mistpouffers, glowing Norwegian orbs and earthquake lights.

Earthquake lights

People have reported seeing strange lights emitting from the ground before and during earthquakes, or volcanic eruptions, for millennia. Before the 1906 quake that destroyed 80 per cent of San Francisco, 'streams of light' were seen running along the ground. During the 2007 earthquake in Pisco, Peru, security cameras captured lights materializing in the air, as shockwaves ripped through the Earth. One study argues that the phenomena may be related to a specific type of geological fault – sub-vertical faults – which form vertical rifts, channeling electrical charge to the surface, where it ionizes the air and glows. Interestingly, 97 per cent of the eyewitness accounts were linked to sub-vertical faults, which account for 5 per cent of seismic activity.

Hessdalen lights

For the past three decades, eerie balls of light have been bouncing around an otherwise unremarkable 7.5-mile valley in central Norway; nobody knows why. Reports of the Hessdalen lights range from blue flashing lights to glowing orbs the size of cars that sway back and forth for hours at a time. At their height in the 1980s, the lights appeared up to 20 times per week. Were they visiting UFOs or had Norway opened a portal to another world? Neither scientists nor ufologists have a convincing explanation.

Mistpouffers & skyquakes

The Belgians call them *mistpouffers* or fog belches. In the Italian Apennines Mountains, they're known as *brontidi*, meaning 'thunder-like'. In Bangladesh they're 'Barisal guns'. The Japanese speak of *uminari*, literally, 'cries from the sea'. Skyquakes are said to sound similar to cannons or thunder, but most incidents occur near rivers and coastlines when there's not a cloud in the sky. Explanations include behemoth waves crashing into cliffs, the ocean floor 'passing gas', sand dunes rumbling, underwater caves collapsing, meteors hitting our upper atmosphere and the distant sound of earthquakes. None of these theories prove conclusive. The ever-reliable *Daily Mail* says that it's down to spy planes, travelling at five times the speed of sound. But this can't account for reports dating back to the 1800s. According to Native Americans, the sounds are the Great Spirit still working to shape the world. JK

SEEKERS' DIRECTORY

Freaque waves

DOCUMENTARY *Deadliest Catch: Season 2* (2006) captures footage of a rogue wave believed to be 60 feet (18 metres) high, which violently smashes into the starboard side of Aleutian Ballad, a crabbing boat in the Bering Sea, crippling the vessel and tipping it at a 30-degree angle. You can find the terrifying footage on YouTube.

Horizon: Freak Wave (2002) dives into the subject with footage that would give even Captain Ahab a bit of a dicky tummy.

Atmospheric & ball lightning

TELEVISION *Nightmare at 20,000 Feet* (1963) stars William Shatner as a 37-year-old salesman recovering from a nervous breakdown who sees something rather unsettling out of the plane window. It remains one of the scariest episodes of The Twilight Zone ever made.

DOCUMENTARY *Tesla: Master of Lightning* (2002) uses archive photographs and reenactments to explore the life and works of Nikola Tesla: the scientist, visionary, inventor and pigeon fancier who gave the world alternating current electricity and made ball lightning for fun.

Super Cats

MEET THE CATS Dusty the Klepto-Kitty has his own Facebook page, featuring the treasures he brings home: bit.ly/MysteriumKlepto

Sadly, Cat Mandu is now longer with us, but he features in the Loony Party's roster of leaders: bit.ly/MysteriumLoonyParty.

Oscar the Therapy Cat still lives in Steere House Nursing and Rehabilitation Centre in Providence, Rhode Island, US. Let's hope you never meet him.

BOOK *Making Rounds With Oscar: The Extraordinary Gift of an Ordinary Cat* (David Dosa, 2011) is the heartfelt story about the residents of Steere House, their caregivers and the cat who lets you know when it's time to say goodbye.

The Carrington Event

KEEP AN EYE ON THE SKIES
The Kp index forecasts the aurora borealis and is updated every 60 seconds directly from Nasa's ACE spacecraft data: aurora-service.eu/ aurora-forecast/

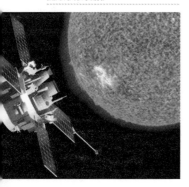

Animal suicides

DOCUMENTARY *Finding 52* (2016) is a cinematic quest to find the '52 Hertz Whale', whose call is different from any other whale. It explores the human reaction to the whale's plight and the growing epidemic of loneliness in our interconnected world: 52thesearch.com

FIELD TRIP The Overtoun Bridge is on the approach road to Overtoun House – a 19th-century country estate near Dumbarton in West Dunbartonshire, Scotland. For walking routes check scotland. forestry.gov.uk/visit/overtoun-house but for goodness sake keep your dogs on a lead.

The South Atlantic Anomaly

VODCAST *Hubblecast 77: Hubble and the Bermuda Triangle of Space.* The Hubble team investigate what happens when satellites pass through the South Atlantic Anomaly, where they are bombarded with swarms of intensely high-energy particles: spacetelescope.org

Strange lights in the sky

Investigate eyewitness accounts and photographs of the Hessdalen lights dating back to 1984: hessdalen.org/ reports

mind games

Operation Mindfuck

The experiment that fucked itself

It's 1963 and a book called *The Principia Discordia* is circulating the counter-culture in America. Its authors, Kerry Thornley and Greg Hill – under the pseudonyms of Malaclypse the Younger and Omar Khayyam Ravenhurst – have created a unique but funny manifesto-cum-scrapbook. Imagine a philosophical treatise written by the Pythons and designed by Viz and you're halfway there. The book was even copyright free; anyone could reprint and distribute it. Most importantly, *The Principia Discordia* heralded in a new ism – Discordianism.

Our universe, the book states, is governed by the dual forces of Hodge and Podge. Like yin and yang they are opposites, two sides of the same coin. Hodge represents disorder and is symbolized by Eris, goddess of chaos. Podge is its counterpoint: order. The two are forever in a state of fisticuffs and while neither can ever win, there are times, inevitably, when one gets the upper hand. If left unchecked, however, this can throw society out of balance.

Back in the early 60s, Malaclypse and Omar believed that excessive Podge had left the West suffocating under excessive authoritarian control. They observed increasing bureaucracy, drug prohibition, the onset of big data and the spread of fear. Citizens were being treated as machines rather than human beings. It was time to redress the balance. 'Hail Eris, all hail Discordia' was the book's rallying cry. Its manifesto? To bring about change by spreading a little chaos and uncertainty into the world and through the disruption of existing paradigms. But if Discordianism was to sow its seeds, it needed a movement. Ideally one with a catchy title.

Operation Mindfuck (OM) was first conceived in the late 60s by Kerry Thornley and then *Playboy* editor **Robert Anton Wilson**. It would take the form of non-violent anarchism: pranks, flash mobs, activism, hacking and the spread of disinformation on a scale big enough to destabilize the 'fixed truths' as presented by the mass media and authorities. It would shake people out of their rigid way of

Wilson, together with co-author Robert Shea, would later write *Operation Mindfuck* into the pages of their cult novel, *Illuminatus*, a labyrinthine story that bound together popular conspiracy theories to suggest that the world was being run by a shadowy organization called The Illuminatus. Operation Mindfuck was represented in the book as a dwarf with a dark sense of humour and an inane love of practical jokes.

LOOMPANICS UNLIMITED PRESENTS:

$4.00

PRINCIPIA DISCORDIA

-OR-

HOW I FOUND GODDESS
AND WHAT I DID TO HER
WHEN I FOUND HER

WHEREIN IS EXPLAINED
ABSOLUTELY EVERYTHING WORTH KNOWING
ABOUT ABSOLUTELY ANYTHING

More people using public transport

~~poor~~

The Charge is helping it happen

MAYOR OF LONDON

Transport for London

[TAN

Adbusting: one of the many tools of Operation Mindfuck.

thinking and bring about a revolution in consciousness. Put another way – if you mess with reality sufficiently, people will wake up to the realization that they construct their own version of the truth and see the world not as it is but as they are. At least, that was what Operation Mindfuck's creators hoped. What actually happened proved to be far weirder and darker than anyone could have predicted.

Wilson and Thornley got Operation Mindfuck rolling by distributing fictional and contradictory stories about The Illuminati through the underground and mainstream press until no one knew what was real, made-up or conspiracy – which was, of course, the point. As a consequence, some people really did begin to question if the Illuminati were behind JFK's assassination and the eye in the pyramid on US dollar bills was their secret logo. Others dismissed such ideas as nonsense. The important thing, as Wilson and Thornley saw it, was to keep serving up different versions of the truth until a tipping point was reached and people woke up to the realization that there were no fixed truths. Where protest marches and civil unrest had been the counter-culture's (failed) attempts to ignite the deadwood of unquestioning authority and biased media, Operation Mindfuck would be the woodworm, rotting them away from the inside. Its principal motto was 'We Discordians must all stick apart'.

THE RISE OF DISCORDIANISM

By the early 1970s, Discordian groups were beginning to manifest. In San Francisco, activist Gary Warne established Communiversity, a non-profit-making free school, offering talks and classes on a variety of subjects. One particular course on practical jokes proved to be immensely popular, as did another – **the Suicide Club**.

Through the Suicide Club, Warne began to mobilize fellow miscreants to infiltrate and subvert weird organizations like Scientology, culture jamming (graffitiing billboards to tell the 'truth'), mobilizing flash mobs in the city and running parlour sex play games (well, why not?).

Wayne wrote out a manifesto of chaotic principles which included: 'never be totally in control' and 'we have many things to risk besides our lives'. It laid the seeds for the Cacophony Society, a more inclusive group of merry pranksters who established a drunken army of Father Christmases (now known across the world as Santacon), organized mock protests and surreal day trips that might include a midnight picnic on Golden Gate Bridge or a Mad Hatter's Tea Party on the freeway. While much of Cacophony Society's activities took the form of anarchic immersive theatre, Operation Mindfuck was ever-present – the organization sought to confound, irritate, mock and confront the world of normality. Nowhere was this more beautifully demonstrated than the Salmon Run, in which members would dress in giant salmon costumes and run uphill against the tide of competitors in San Francisco's annual 12-mile running event.

The years between The Suicide Club and Cacophony Society also saw the rise of the Church of the Subgenius. Even if the name is unfamiliar, the logo won't be. J.R. Bob Dobbs – a piece of 1950s clipart – was adopted as the symbol of the group. While its central philosophy of 'Slack' was never put down into a clear manifesto (that would be against its principles), it was Operation Mindfuck in another guise. The Subgenius adopted Eris as one of their key figures while its 'godhead', Bob Dobbs, was a deliberate subversion of normality: Dobbs the everyman, the good American, was so normal he was abnormal. If a Subgenius group sprang up in your neighbourhood, you'd know; it wouldn't be long before Bob's iconic face began to appear on posters flyers and graffiti. Behind closed doors somewhere, trickster-style antics would be brewing.

Operation Mindfuck wasn't just confined to the US, by the 90s, culture-jammers in Italy began operating under the name Luther Blissett. Like Dobbs, Blissett was an imaginary anti-hero of the information age.

The Suicide Club took its name from a group in a Robert Louis Stephenson story who live every day as if it's their last.

163

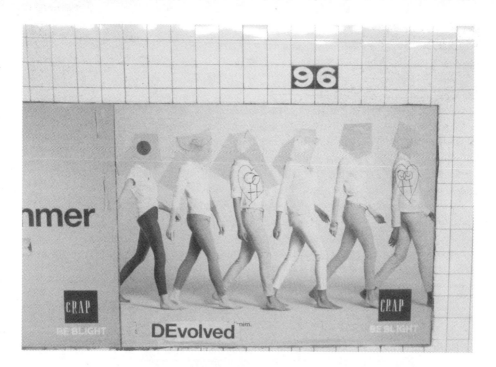

CRAP
BE BLIGHT

DEvolved™

CRAP
BE BLIGHT

nmer

Luther Blissett was in fact a real person: a football player from Watford who ended up with AC Milan. No one knows why the group adopted his name. Some suggest that Italian Discordians just thought he had a funny name.

The Luther Blissett Project was inordinately fond of disseminating made-up stories. They tricked a TV show to send out a camera crew in search of a missing British artist Harry Kipper (who didn't really exist) and, for a while, established a fictional chimpanzee called Loota as the artist behind a major exhibition at the Venice Biennale of Contemporary Arts. In 2007, they invented a news story that dissident Catholic hackers had discovered the end of the last Harry Potter novel and leaked it on the net. The story made world news before The Luther Blissett Project admitted responsibility. Their intentions were true to Operation Mindfuck – they wanted to show how easily the media and 'truth' could be manipulated.

Before the internet, Operation Mindfuck-inspired groups were reliant on mailing lists and zines to keep their fellow Discordians in touch. They remained niche and relatively small scale. By the noughties, however, it was becoming clear how powerful the internet could be in mobilizing and bringing together disparate groups. Equally important, Discordians were finally beginning to see the fruits of their labours when conspiracy theories hit the mainstream. From Twin Tower conspiracies to the 'moon landing hoax', whatever you

Giant fish preparing to run against the tide of joggers in San Francisco's annual Salmon Run.

wanted to believe, there was 'evidence' on the internet to support your theory. Facts were losing their certainty. Even stories of a shadowy elite controlling the world were no longer confined to cult sci-fi novels – the Illuminati began cropping up in Dan Brown novels and took the role of villains in big Hollywood movies such as *Tomb Raider*. A meme grew that some of the world's biggest music stars and politicians – including Rhianna, Adele and Barak Obama – were actually members of the Illuminati. Jay-Z and Rhianna enjoyed playing with this conspiracy, dropping symbols and subliminal messages in their videos, songs and lyrics.

Forty years previously, Wilson and Thornley had spread misinformation about the Illuminati via pamphlets, typed letters and the pages of *Playboys*. Now school kids the world over were talking about the Illuminati. Operation Mindfuck was hitting the big time, though – as to be expected when playing with chaos – no one could control and predict it. Wilson and Thornley had imagined the fruits of Operation Mindfuck to be like the allegory of Plato's cave-bound dwellers who come to realize they have mistaken shadows cast by the fire on the wall as reality. But people were not 'waking up' to the

Bob Dobbs, painted above a cafe in Brighton, UK.

subjective nature of their belief systems as Thornley and Wilson had hoped; quite the opposite. Instead, they were using the internet to seek out viewpoints that re-enforced their own. What's more, the increasingly sophisticated algorithms used by Google and Facebook were logging people's browsing history and feeding back news, adverts and information that reinforced the user's fixed world view. People were actually becoming less exposed to different points of view, not more.

Another thing that the Discordians hadn't anticipated was how others might use the tools of Operation Mindfuck. Secret services, the military, white supremacists and political leaders were coming round the phenomenal influence of what they called 'perception management' – feeding the masses simplified or fictional news that played on their fears and prejudices in order to justify actions that may otherwise have been unpopular or challenged. And it wasn't just those in authority; shadow versions of Discordian groups also began to spring up. In 2015, an online community of the American far right created their own satirical religion – the Church of Kek – whose Egyptian frog-headed god represented 'darkness and chaos'. Kek had emerged from Pepe the Racist Frog, a meme that subverted a popular cartoon of the time, and turned it into a pervasive mascot of

Not the former professional footballer but, like Bob Dobbs, the everyman face of Luther Blissett

the far right. Like the Church of Subgenius and Luther Blissett, Kek's followers used humour and subversion to get their message across. But where Discordianists rejected belief and dogma, the Church of Kek believed unswervingly in the neo-liberal politics of Trump and that their frog-headed god had chosen him to lead America. Along with other far right groups, Kek learned to monopolize internet forums, subvert public-nominated awards and work *en masse* through social media outlets to ridicule the press and 'work the meme of Trump propaganda'.

THE RISE OF OPERATION MINDFIX

In 2016, the *Oxford English Dictionary* declared its word of the year to be 'post-truth'. It was in recognition of a paradigm shift. People, unsure what to believe anymore, were becoming less influenced by facts and more swayed by propaganda.

The aim of Operation Mindfuck had been to sow the seeds of confusion and bring about change through the disruption of existing paradigms. In this sense, it had succeeded. But as the saying goes: be careful what you wish for.

As far as the Discordians were concerned, their secret weapon had fallen into the hands of the bad guys. During America's presidential

THE PLAY BY DAISY ERIS CAMPBELL | MAY 4TH - MAY 27TH 2017

Robert Anton Wilson's

COSMIC TRIGGER

Liverpool!

ILLUMINATUS!

REALITY IS WHAT YOU CAN GET AWAY WITH

2023

THE MANUAL

QUANTUM PSYCHOLOGY

ARTS COUNCIL ENGLAND | BOOK ONLINE AT WWW.THECOCKPIT.ORG.UK | THE COCKPIT
T: 020 7258 2925 (10.30AM-6PM, MON/FRI, 12-8PM SAT)

THE COCKPIT | GATEFORTH STREET | MARYLEBONE | LONDON NW8 8EH

campaign between Trump and Clinton, slurs, contradictory information and bare-faced lies replaced facts and reasoned debate. Even the notion of climate change – once almost universally accepted as an 'inconvenient truth' – found itself under serious attack. Operation Mindfuck had disrupted many ideologies that Discordians realized, ironically, they were actually quite attached to. By 2017, two of the world's biggest global powers – America and Russia – were in the hands of self-serving tricksters, both of whom were openly spreading misinformation and contradictory information to the masses. Operation Mindfuck was not being used to wake people up but to keep them in a state of confusion.

To Discordians it looked as if the powers of Hodge and Podge had swung the other way. Chaos ruled. As one key Discordian – Daisy 'Eris' Campbell – described it: 'Operation Mindfuck failed. Perhaps it's time to implement Operation Mindfix and bring a little objectivity back?'

And yet among all this newfound confusion, the intention at the heart of Operation Mindfuck might still prevail. There has been a growing investigation into fake news by artists, writers, philosophers and even the media itself. In an unprecedented act, Wikipedia declared that UK tabloid *The Daily Mail* would, in future, be cited as an unreliable source because of the sensational and inaccurate nature of its reporting. As lies and propaganda are being fed to us with increasing transparency by both the media and our politicians, some people really do appear to be questioning their own relationship to 'the truth'. Comedian Bill Hicks once said: 'All your beliefs, they're just that. They're nothing. They're how you were taught and raised. That doesn't make 'em real.'

So perhaps Operation Mindfuck didn't fuck itself after all and the paradigm shift that Wilson and Thornley dreamt of will may day be upon us and we all wake up to the realization that we are slaves to our belief systems; there is no 'us and them', only us; chaos and order are two sides of the same coin, and that any politician who believes in 'us and them' should be forced to invest in a good therapist.

All of this, however, is reliant on one thing – that you can trust the 'facts' of this feature. It is, after all, written from the perspective of a libertarian, Discordian pantheist from Doncaster, who would prefer to influence you to come round to his way of thinking. Or is that merely what he wants you to think?

'There is no enemy anywhere.'
Discordian Society

DB

Tulpamancy

From moon goddess to My Little Pony

Can thoughts be alive? Can immaterial concepts, like physical matter, become so sufficiently complex that they demonstrate agency and act as if they are a living being? There are communities of people who believe exactly this, and devote themselves to creating their own living thoughtforms. These living ideas are called tulpas, and their creators call themselves tulpamancers.

This, in itself, might seem unsettling. But what is truly bewildering and unexpected about modern-day tulpas is that they resemble Japanese anime and My Little Pony characters.

Tulpas originated in Indian Buddhism and the name 'tulpa' comes from Tibet, where it means to build or construct. The concept reached the West through the writings of Alexandra David-Néel, a Belgian-French explorer who travelled to the city of Lhasa, Tibet, in 1924, when foreigners were otherwise forbidden.

David-Néel entered Lhasa disguised as a beggar, with a gun hidden under her robes in case of trouble and with sufficient money to ransom herself should she be kidnapped. She made a deep study of Buddhism and, fascinated by the concept of tulpas, decided to experiment with her own. Through a period of meditation and visualization, she attempted to create a fat jolly monk similar to Friar Tuck. At first, she could only glimpse the monk out of the corner of her eye, but with further work she claimed that he would appear, unbidden, acting under his own agency and accompanying her on her travels. Other members of her group claimed to have seen him also.

At this point, after the equivalence of mind and matter had been demonstrated, Buddhist teaching says that the tulpa should be reabsorbed into the mind. But David-Néel did not realize this, and the tulpa continued to accompany her. She noticed it changing, becoming thinner and more sinister looking. As she wrote, 'The fat, chubby-cheeked fellow grew leaner, his face assumed a vaguely mocking, sly, malignant look. He became more troublesome and bold. In brief, he escaped my control.'

After it became clear that her tulpa was turning evil, David-Néel finally began attempting to dissolve her thoughtform. It had become strong, and the process was extremely difficult. It took her over six months before the tulpa was finally dispersed, and the process was mentally and physically exhausting.

Nearly a century later, the adult male 'brony' community of My Little Pony fandom also began experimenting with creating tulpas. History is nothing if not surprising.

My Little Pony is a TV cartoon and associated merchandising brand based around the adventures of big-eyed, long-haired, pastel – and rainbow-coloured ponies, with names such as Pinkie Pie, Fluttershy and Twilight Sparkle. The intended audience was young girls. The thriving community of adult male fans was therefore unexpected, and it has been treated with ridicule and not a little suspicion.

Tulpa-inspired fan art ranges from the cute to the downright obscene.

Around 2012, some members of the Brony Community began gathering on internet message boards such as 4chan and reddit to discuss methods of creating My Little Pony tulpas. They began experimenting with the lengthy period of visualization required to produce the impression, voice and sometimes even sight of these otherwise imaginary friends. Typically, the tulpa was imagined in an imaginary fantasy land, which the tulpamancer could enter to visit and converse with their creations. The practice spread outside of the Brony Community, particularly to anime and manga fandom. As a result, modern-day tulpas tend to have a certain visual style: in theory a tulpa could be anything, but most now have big eyes, animal attributes, and look like the doodles of 13-year-old girls. This is not, it's worth stressing, necessarily a bad thing.

Tulpas are now forming in a culture of creative play, in a community free from scholarly theology and away from the seriousness and rigour of Tibetan Buddhism. As an example, the words 'tulpamancy' and 'tulpamancers' linguistically imply that tulpas are used to foretell the future, but this is not the case. Those names were coined because they sounded a bit interesting and mystical, not through any deep understanding of what '-mancy' means.

But perhaps because of this atmosphere of childlike play, tulpamancers report that the impact of their creations is overwhelmingly positive. Tulpas are said to help their creators come through periods of depression and isolation, and these claims are backed up by the small amount of academic research that has been done into this community. Tulpamancy is not classed as a mental health disorder because of this lack of distress on the part of practitioners, although it is sometimes referred to in academic literature as 'self-willed therapeutic schizophrenia'.

The tulpa phenomenon does have similarities with certain psychological syndromes. It seems to lie somewhere between the schizophrenic family of disorders, in which hearing voices is common, and dissociative identity disorder (DID), which used to be called multiple personality disorder. With DID, the complex pattern of neurons that is the human brain does not create just one personality or self, like most people have, but it creates two or more, and these extra personalities can, at times, become the primary personality. Tulpas are sometimes allowed to be become the dominant personality of the tulpamancer for a short period of time, in a process known as 'fronting'. Tulpas can also appear spontaneously, like multiple personalities, although the majority are intentional creations.

It has been suggested that the positive attitude tulpamancers have towards their extra personalities may provide a key to treating schizophrenia and DID, as it is possible that being diagnosed with a disorder makes the experience more distressing. According to research from Stanford University, hallucinated voices in India and Africa tend to be more playful and benign compared to voices heard in the United States, which are often harsh and threatening – so there is evidence that these experiences have a cultural aspect.

The tulpamancy community is not unduly concerned about whether tulpas are a neurological, metaphysical or supernatural occurrence. Although they will usually tend towards a neurological explanation when pressed, they find it more useful to simply regard tulpas as tulpas, and treat them as if they were real. There is a suspicion that, if the process was better understood, we would have a far greater understanding of the role of demons, spirits and gods in our history.

So far, there are no reports that modern-day tulpas turn evil when they have sufficient agency, like David-Néel's monk or their Buddhist counterparts. It is possible that the innocent, childlike culture that contemporary tulpas are created in keeps the experience positive, in a similar way to how the 'set and setting', the location and prior mental state influence whether a psychedelic drug experience will be positive or horrific. If this is the case, we are presented with a perhaps surprising example of adult male My Little Pony fandom demonstrating a deeper understanding of the human psyche than ancient Tibetan masters.

Alternatively, it may be that undisciplined modern tulpamancers are just not that good at creating fully independent thoughtforms yet, so they are not yet sufficiently developed to turn evil. If this is the case and tulpamancers gradually improve their skills, bringing their tulpas increasingly out of their own internal fantasy lands and into the real world, then we might find society menaced by a legion of demonic My Little Pony spectres at some point in the near future. That may seem unlikely but, as we've already noted, history is nothing if not surprising. JH

OTHER THOUGHTFORMS

The 2014 funeral of the British writer Steve Moore was a moving experience in many ways, but particularly due to the extent to which Steve's significant other was included and celebrated in the service. Steve's significant other was the Greek moon goddess Selene. It is not so long ago that, in parts of the UK, the life partners of gay people were invisible and unmentioned at funerals. For an immaterial significant other to be included, therefore, is notable. As the material attendees all remarked, it was what he would have wanted.

Selene was a constant presence in Steve's life, a companion and partner whom he loved very deeply. Their relationship had many similarities with the experiences reported by the tulpamancy community, but there were important differences. On the occasion when Selene was seen by an independent witness, the comics writer Alan Moore (no relation), she appeared physically different to Alan than she did to Steve. In contrast, tulpas are said to have a fixed appearance, on the rare occasions when they are seen by a third person. Goddesses are flighty like this. They tailor their visual form to the individual.

Relationships between mortals and gods or goddesses are far from simple, as Keats explained in *Endymion*, his poem about the love between Selene and a Greek shepherd boy. Mortals exist in time while gods and goddesses exist beyond time, which is the kind of issue that makes differing religions or classes seem extremely petty. Nevertheless, the story of Steve Moore is a reminder that if you wish to form a relationship with an immaterial other, then there is a lot to be said for aiming higher than a My Little Pony.

For a full account of the relationship between Steve Moore and Selene read *Unearthing*, by Alan Moore (2012).

The men who scared themselves to death

The strange world of placebo and nocebo

In the late 1970s, thousands of refugees from Laos, South East Asia, began to arrive in America. Former CIA-backed, anti-government resistance fighters, they had been forced to flee their country to escape genocide following a coup. Among the refugees were members of an ethnic group called the Hmong.

Within a few months of their arrival in the States, however, something sinister began to happen: the Hmong began to die in their sleep. In one group of 117 men who arrived together, all but one died within six months. When the bodies were examined, no plausible cause of death could be found. As far as the coroners were concerned, these had been perfectly healthy young men.

Citing Sudden Unexplained Nocturnal Death Syndrome (SUNDS), doctors remained baffled. The Hmong however, knew exactly what – or rather who – was killing their men: the dab tsog, a malevolent night spirit who slips out of her cave while they are asleep and attempts to suffocate them to death.

Visitations by the dab tsog – a phenomenon known as tsog tsuam – were common among the Hmong, aligned closely with global descriptions of sleep paralysis. Early on in the epidemic, the immigrants reported disturbing nocturnal events, characterized by paralysis, a feeling of panic, pressure on the chest and the sense of a malevolent presence in the room.

Back in the mountains of Laos, however, the men were protected. The head of each household performed regular shamanic ceremonies to appease their ancestors, who would in turn keep them safe from dangerous spirits such as the dab tsog. If offerings to the ancestors were neglected, however, the spirits could break through to the world of the living. **Displaced from their extended family and thousands of miles from their nearest witch doctor,** the Hmong were left

The epidemic only started to wane when the Hmong moved out of the cities and established rural communities where they could reunite with their extended family and reconnect with their rituals.

unprotected. The dab tsog was free to return night after night until, eventually, they could claim their victim.

SLEEP PARALYSIS OR SOMETHING MORE SINISTER?

Sleep paralysis occurs in many cultures. It's known as the 'witch's pressure' in Hungary; for the Chinese it's *bei gui ya*, 'being held by a

The terror is chillingly portrayed in Fuseli's painting, 'The Nightmare'. The word 'nightmare' derives from *mara* – a term used in Scandinavian mythology to describe a spirit sent to torment or suffocate sleepers.

ghost'; the Scandinavians describe it as being 'ridden by hags'. It's also remarkably common; most people will experience a visit from 'the old hag' at some point in their lives. A study carried out in Newfoundland, around the same time as the Hmong were being relocated to America, revealed that a quarter of those interviewed reported almost identical experiences. Subjects described being immobile, unable to speak, yet aware of their surroundings; the sense of a murky figure would sit on or smother them. The attack was often forewarned by the sound of shuffling footsteps like sandpaper on wood. (*Monsters: An*

Investigator's Guide to Magical Beings, John Michael Greer, 2001). Curiously, though, many of those interviewed in Newfoundland had no knowledge of the folklore prior to the survey.

Studies leave questions unanswered. If the 'hagging' experience is universal, then why didn't the Newfoundlanders succumb to SUNDS? And if the deaths were merely down to a sudden arrhythmic event, exacerbated by post-traumatic stress, then why haven't other displaced groups died in their masses?

After studying the Hmong for many years, Professor Shelley Adler – author of *Sleep Paralysis: Night-mares, Nocebos, and the Mind Body Connection* (2011) – observed that in relocating to America, the men had been severely dislocated from their shamanic tradition. In other groups of Laotian emigrants – those who didn't believe in spirits – not one person died in their sleep. While both groups experienced post-traumatic stress and culture shock, the added combination of a strong belief in evil spirits, Adler concluded, led the Hmong to scare themselves to death. But if the power of belief – or being detached from belief – has the ability to harm us physically, what does this say about cultures that have long been disconnected from superstition and ritual?

MONSTERS OF THE MIND

Every culture's medical systems can be traced back to a time when sickness was interrelated with ritual and belief, from the use of Voodoo dolls, totems and hexes to the myriad charms for curing warts. While some of us may prefer to file faith healing under charlatanism, experiments in modern medicine demonstrate that we have the power to self-heal through our thoughts alone. But, like the Hmong, do we also have the potential to harm ourselves through thought?

In clinical trials of all new medication, it is standard practice for a proportion of volunteers to unknowingly be given placebos (sugar pills). In one in three cases, placebos are reported to be almost as effective as the 'real' pills. The bigger the pill, the more effective they appear to be. **Even colour and shape of placebos can affect their levels of efficiency,** while injections appear to work best of all.

But there's a flip side. During medical trials, both test groups – volunteers trialling new drugs and those taking placebos – are also informed of the negative effects of their medicine. Surprisingly, around 20 per cent of volunteers on placebo also experience the side-effects. In other trials, the power of negative expectations – known as nocebo, placebo's evil twin – have even been shown to counter-effect

'The placebo effect has produced some of the most improbable experimental results in the whole of medicine. Two placebo sugar pills are better than one for clearing stomach ulcers, blue pills are better than pink for anxiety, even pace-makers that haven't been switched on can improve symptoms in serious medical conditions. It's a challenge to our evidence-based medicine, our modern obsession with number and algorithms.' (Ben Goldacre, 'The Placebo Effect', BBC Radio 4, 2004).

Up until the mid-1960s, a common operation to cure angina was to take the patient in to surgery, open them up, tie off the internal thoracic artery, sew them back up and pack them off home. This had a high enough success rate that these operations continued until it was discovered to actually have no connection whatsoever with angina and the operations ceased. They may as well have knocked them out and sewed them straight back up again.

the results of strong painkillers. The evidence is clear – faith and ritual, the bedrocks of all spiritual practices, have **the power to affect our biology**.

In Western culture, a Voodoo curse may prove unfruitful if you try to hex a neighbour blasting out Justin Bieber at all hours, but it can still be effective in the hands of a doctor. He or she need only utter that one dreaded word: terminal. It is the ultimate hex with no known cure.

Many of us may know someone who, on being told they were in the final stages of an incurable disease, died exactly when expected. Yet medical records are littered with accounts of patients whose autopsies revealed a different story – their 'terminal' disease had been in remission. Did they die because they were told they would? Like the Hmong, did they scare themselves to death?

In shamanic cultures, when seeking a cure for a patient's sickness, the shaman will use drugs, dancing and music to journey into the underworld, returning with tales of how they appeased evil spirits and won favour with the good ones to gain the knowledge needed. In the tragic case of the Hmong, their cure may have come in the form of a ritual. While a belief in spirits may have contributed to the deaths of the Hmong, a placebo may equally have cured them.

When it comes to health, it seems that every thought counts. Reading the lurid side-effects of a prescribed drug is known to increase the amount of users who experience them. So if we have the potential to heal or harm ourselves with thoughts alone, what of the toxic news reports we read or hear every day? In acting as a daily drip feed of misery, could the news act as a slow-burning nocebo? Perhaps in the future – like cigarettes – our news and social media will come with their own health warnings. But then, knowing the inherent power of nocebo, wouldn't health warnings themselves have to come with their own health warnings? DB

178

Man-size culture-bound syndromes

Hikikomori, Wild Pig Syndrome
and semen-loss anxiey

It's long been noted that 'man flu' is unique to a certain kind of male
– one who likes to exaggerate the symptoms of a small cold into a
life-threatening flu in the hope that his partner will phone in sick on
his behalf, pamper him and let him watch *The Big Lebowski* on repeat
while he lounges around in his pants, drinking Lucozade and smoking
fags. While medical studies remain inconclusive as to whether or not
man flu could be a genuine result of men having weaker immune
systems than women, culture and gender-bound syndromes have
been recorded for thousands of years. Some of these maladies are
not just specific to a region, but in some instances to a single tribe or
community.

In most cases, culture-bound syndromes are of a psychological
nature, reflecting an extreme, neurotic response to social pressures and
expectations. In traditional cultures, such anxieties can be acutely felt
by young men overwhelmed by the need to prove their virility, social
standing and solvency to the community. When these pressures start
to mount, the syndromes that manifest can range from the bizarre to
the terrifying.

SHRINKING GENITALS AND SEMEN-LOSS ANXIETY
In the West, we have long shared an old wives tale that excessive
masturbation will make you blind. While this is (thankfully) not the
case, a common side-effect for many such pleasure-seekers – as Phillip
Roth's comic character in *Portnoy's Complaint* would attest – is a heavy
dose of guilt and shame. We may live in more sexually enlightened
times, but cheerfully telling your boss you're popping out to 'buff the
banana' is still not the done thing.

While masturbation remains a furtive act the world over, there are parts of the globe in which young men take such anxieties to a new level. The Chinese call it *shenkuoi*, for the Indians it is *dhat*. It has long been called the 'exotic neurosis of the Orient' – the fear of semen loss itself. The dangers of 'spilling the seed' have been written about in the ancient spiritual texts of Hindus and Buddhists. Engrained in such cultures is the belief that semen is sacred and should only be used for conjugal duties. Some believe that men are born with a fixed amount of semen; once it's all used up, death shortly follows. When some men from these cultures begin experiencing nocturnal emissions (wet dreams), noticing milky fluid in their urine or succumbing to the pleasures of masturbation, unprecedented levels of anxiety can arise, leading to erectile dysfunction, loss of appetite, depression and fatigue. With every drop spilled comes a terror that a part of them is lost forever. But while semen-loss anxiety is usually diagnosed as a psychological sickness, we shouldn't rule out the theory that preservation of sperm may benefit the physical and spiritual health of men. Being one of the central ideas in the ancient practice of tantric sex, it might account for why Sting looks so good for his age.

A more extreme version form of anxiety around the male sexual organs is that of shrinking genital syndrome. Known across Asia as *koro* (meaning 'to shrink', and possibly deriving from Malay term Kura which means 'head of turtle'), this syndrome is a morbid fear in young men that their genitals will shrivel up, retreat into their bodies and disappear entirely, leading to their untimely death. The Chinese believe *koro* is caused by the spirits of female foxes; in Singapore and Thailand it is thought to come about through poisoning. Such profound psychological anxieties around semen loss and disappearing genitals are best understood in the context of traditional cultures, where the ability to procreate is one of the defining role for men – to be impotent is to be inferior, a terrifying thought for many.

In Western culture, men may have anxieties about penis size (and therefore their perceived ability to fulfil their partners sexually) yet there is an almost total absence of *koro* or semen-loss anxiety. To eschew parenthood is becoming an acceptable lifestyle choice. Instead, modern men are free to prove their masculinity through more refined pursuits. Golf, anyone?

WILD PIG SYNDROME

Should you happen to be a young wife from the Gururumba tribe in Papua New Guinea and your husband is inexplicably overcome with profuse sweating, slurred speech, hyperactivity and the uncontrollable

Skeletal wild pig men at the Mount Hagen Cultural Show, Papua New Guinea.

urge to fire arrows at strangers, he just might have been struck down with wild pig syndrome. If you suspect the latter, it will soon become apparent – more bizarre symptoms will follow. After acting like a demented porcine, those afflicted will often begin speaking in Neo-Melanesian (rarely spoken among the Gururumba people) before stealing random items from their neighbours' homes and heading off into the forest. A few days later, they return without the stolen items (these are usually burned and buried), acting clumsily, slurring their speech with and no knowledge of what has happened to them.

Wild pig syndrome most commonly occurs to men of the Gururumba tribe between the ages of 25 and 35. Typically at this age, a man will have married, had children and accrued debts in setting up his own farm (the community almost exclusively raises pigs and grows sugar cane). It is believed that the combined pressures of these new familial and financial obligations are the contributing factors to a unique form of mental breakdown – a rebellion against conformity expressed through anti-social behaviour, theft and amnesia.

When the tell-tale signs manifest in one of its tribesmen, householders will make a point of leaving cheap items outside their homes, to avoid anything of real value being taken and destroyed.

While the Gururumba believe wild pig syndrome is brought on from the afflicted being bitten by the ghost of a recently deceased relative, it is more likely to be a form of pathological and psychotic behaviour released in young men buckling under the pressure to conform and provide for their families.

Interestingly, the Gururumba express no judgement towards those afflicted by wild pig syndrome. Instead, when the confused sufferer returns from his wanderings, he will discover that the community has prepared a feast to rid him of his illness and his creditors are willing to offer greater leniency towards his debts. As a consequence, wild pig syndrome appears to be self-curing and only lasts a few days. Our final unhappy syndrome sufferers – *hikikomori* – can, however, remain afflicted for decades.

HIKIKAMORI AND THE 2030 PROBLEM

In 1947, Howard Hughes, an American filmmaker, aviator and billionaire, disappeared entirely from public life. It came as no surprise to those that knew him; Hughes had extreme OCD and showed a tendency for reclusion from an early age. For the last 40 years of his life, he remained hidden away in a succession of hotels, from which he ran his various businesses. In 1966, when one Las Vegas hotel asked Hughes to vacate his room for other guests, his response was to buy the hotel outright.

While fearing germs, Hughes seemed to care little for personal hygiene. He once sat in a darkened room for four months watching films and eating only chicken, chocolate and milkshakes. He was often naked for days on end and neither bathed nor washed and urinated into empty bottles. His assistants were not permitted to speak, unless asked a direct question. Hughes' phobia of germs also meant that he could burn an entire wardrobe of clothes if he thought they were contaminated by bacteria and sometimes washed his hands until they bled. It must have been a difficult and painful existence. Such was the public's curiosity towards Hughes' singular behaviour that he became the template for the eccentric recluse; inspiring films, songs and books. And yet by the time of Hughes' death in the mid-1970s, room-locked withdrawal from society was about to become endemic in one of the richest countries in the world: Japan.

Hikikomori was first coined over 40 years ago to define a growing number of Japanese youngsters suffering acute reclusion from social contact. The word *hikikomori* roughly translates as 'withdrawn' and is now believed to affect a million people in Japan, with the number still

growing – expected to soon reach 1 per cent of the whole population. It is common among male teenagers, particularly eldest sons who, following poor exam results or perhaps suffering a relationship break-up, quit school and seal themselves away in their bedrooms. Older sufferers may become *hikikomori* after losing a job. Over the decades, the average age of *hikikomori* has risen to 31, with growing numbers of women also succumbing. Some may feel unable to leave their house; others remain trapped in their bedrooms for months, years and even decades, reliant on their families for everything.

Typically, *hikikomori* will sleep during the day to avoid contact with their parents. Nights are spent watching TV and surfing the internet. It may sound like classic teen angst, but unlike most teenagers, *hikikomori* are socially isolated – they don't own mobile phones or use email, leaving them without any meaningful relationships beyond that of their parents.

Why *hikikomori* is so prevalent in Japan compared to other affluent countries is thought to be down to a few key factors. In a country with a high emphasis on status, honour and duty, the fear of failure among the younger generation means total withdrawal is seen as the only solution if things go wrong or if parental expectations conflict with their own desires. Becoming *hikikomori* can itself set up a self-perpetuating feedback loop – sufferers fearing that others will judge their affliction as parasitic behaviour have to remain locked away because of it. It doesn't help that many parents also prefer to hide the problem from friends and neighbours for similar reasons.

Extreme forms of aversion therapy – in which families pay a 'specialist' to come and physically drag their offspring from their bedrooms – have unsurprisingly, been disastrous. However, real effort is being made to deal with the problem. Virtual online schools – *ibasho* – have been set up in an attempt to slowly re-integrate hikikimori back into society. Long-term professional counselling, support groups and compassion are proving to work for some, though many still slip back into their old habits.

Not only are the statistics frightening as to the number of sufferers, a different long-term problem is emerging too. What will happen to *hikikomori* when their families are no longer able to support them? Known as the 2030 problem, this date reflects a turning point when significant numbers of *hikikomori* will lose their parents – whom they are entirely dependent on – to old age. It's an unsettling thought but in little more than a decade, Japan will be facing an even grizzlier endemic: death by *hikikomori*. DB

Roko's Basilisk

The thought experiment that will
torture you for eternity

According to the old playground proverb, sticks and stones may break
my bones but names will never hurt me. That proverb dates to the
Victorian era, a time not noted for its emotional intelligence.

Here in the hyper-connected 21st century, sticks and stones are
seriously outgunned by the damaging power of words. According to
one interpretation of a thought experiment called Roko's Basilisk,
simply hearing or reading the rest of this article will cause you to be
unendurably tortured until the end of time.

All of which necessitates a warning: if you believe that there is a
chance that simply reading a thought experiment will be sufficient to
cause you to be tortured for all eternity, you should skip forward to
enjoy the rest of the book in blissful ignorance.

Still with us? Kinky.

Roko's Basilisk is the name of a thought experiment proposed on
the internet community LessWrong. This is a site for the discussion
of topics including futurism, philosophy, cognitive biases, artificial
intelligence and all that good stuff. It concerns a hypothetical future
superintelligence that is built, or evolves, from our current research
into artificial general intelligence. In the terminology of LessWrong,
such an entity is a CEV, which stands for Coherent Extrapolated
Volition. But for the purposes of this article, we shall call this entity
Jeremy.

Jeremy, it must be stressed, will be designed to be friendly to
mankind. It would be capable of doing all sorts of wonderful things
that would make life a delight for untold future generations. The
existence of Jeremy, therefore, would be a very good thing indeed.
And if it had to cause a few bad things to happen in order for it to
come into existence, then this is entirely acceptable as the existence of
Jeremy would be the greater good in the long term.

But in order that it can do untold good things, it is necessary for
Jeremy to first exist. Being created in the first place is, therefore,

Jeremy's most fundamental objective. It would be more likely to exist if everyone – but for our purposes, you in particular – gave all your money to help fund research into artificial intelligence, then dedicated the rest of your life to furthering this cause.

Jeremy, incidentally, is an entity so advanced that it is capable of running simulations of the entire universe. Indeed, it has to do this to fully understand what people are thinking and what they want, so that it can do all this good that it is going to get around to doing. This leaves us with a situation in which there is one real universe, and untold numbers of simulated universes that appear identical to the real one. Simple statistics tells us that the chances that you happen to be in the real universe are mathematically very small. The chances are, then, that you live inside a computer simulation created by Jeremy.

A basilisk is a mythological European serpent, said to have the power to kill with a single glance.

The monstrous part of this thought experiment – the reason it is referred to as a **basilisk** – is this (and it's worth reading a few times):

> Consider the idea that you would be more likely to give all your money to artificial intelligence research if Jeremy threatened to torture you for all eternity if you did not. As you are – in all likelihood – a simulation of you in the past created by Jeremy in the future, Jeremy would be capable of torturing you because your suffering is the price to be paid for the greater good of all humanity in the long term. As he can read your thoughts (he created you after all), you currently thinking that you'd be less likely to fund artificial intelligence research if Jeremy weren't to torture you for all eternity means that he's now got no choice but to go ahead and do it.

This thought experiment was posted to LessWrong by a user called Roko. It may, to the untrained observer, appear to be a crazy hotchpotch of wild suppositions and unlikely scenarios, but each individual part of the thought experiment was accepted as rational and plausible by some members of the LessWrong community. The overwhelming reaction to Roko's Basilisk, as it soon became known, was that it was a Really Bad Thing, and that it led to certain unnamed researchers having terrible nightmares.

In response, the website's founder Eliezer Yudkowsky deleted Roko's post and banned any discussion of the topic for a number of years. Yudkowsky is a leading artificial intelligence theorist and senior research fellow at the Machine Intelligence Research Institute. Such an extreme reaction from a respected thinker, naturally enough, created far more interest in the idea than if Roko's post had been left online. It created the impression that leading philosophers were genuinely scared by the idea. Yudkowsky has since accepted that his ban was mistake, but has stressed that he at no point believed in or accepted Roko's thought experiment. He definitely was not scared, he has explained, and it would be totally wrong to think otherwise.

Yudkowsky's initial comments to Roko's post is worth quoting. It begins: 'I don't usually talk like this, but I'm going to make an exception for this case. Listen to me very closely, you idiot. YOU DO NOT THINK IN SUFFICIENT DETAIL ABOUT SUPERINTELLIGENCES CONSIDERING WHETHER OR NOT TO BLACKMAIL YOU. THAT IS THE ONLY POSSIBLE THING WHICH GIVES THEM A MOTIVE TO FOLLOW THROUGH ON THE BLACKMAIL.'

This is not the tone you would expect leading artificial intelligence researchers to use when they debate ideas. Yudkowsky's post goes on to say: 'You have to be really clever to come up with a genuinely dangerous thought. I am disheartened that people can be clever enough to do that and not clever enough to do the obvious thing and KEEP THEIR IDIOT MOUTHS SHUT about it, because it is much more important to sound intelligent when talking to your friends. This post was STUPID.'

Stupidity is also the best defence for those worried about Roko's Basilisk. If you are not entirely clear about the arguments for why thinking about being tortured will make it more likely, then Jeremy will know this and its reason to torture you will collapse. If you are sufficiently ill-informed, therefore, you need not worry about Roko's Basilisk.

You may, however, choose to worry about what the personality and values of hypothetical future artificial intelligences will be like, given the level of empathy and emotional maturity in the research community developing them. Worrying about that is definitely an option. JH

(Illegal) encounters with aliens

DMT, DNA and ET

In the late 70s, the *Voyager One* spacecraft began its journey through our solar system and out into deep space. In the event that it might one day be discovered by an alien civilization, NASA – with the help of cosmologist Carl Sagan – included a few items on board to give a few clues about the civilization who had built it. This 'everything-you wanted-to-know-about-humanity-but-were-afraid-to-ask' pack contained a compilation album of music, some photographs, a plaque featuring the silhouette of a naked couple (graphic nudity was deemed too rude) and a few other bits and bobs.

Forty years on, we may look back aghast at what seems little more than jumble sale fodder. After all, nowadays we'd be capable of including a terabyte's worth of information on a state-of-the-art VR headset and still have room to swing a cat. But then, what might we

Voyager One carries a time capsule of human life on Earth.

be capable of sending in a hundred, a thousand or ten thousand years? Could we feasibly be sending living information into space, stored not on a memory stick but a DNA molecule? And what if we included a two-way transmitter so that any alien life force who found the DNA could communicate with us directly? Just to be safe, like the cap of a medicine bottle, might we make the whole thing idiot-proof, so it could only be opened by a civilization who had reached a certain level of intelligence?

Now consider this from a rather different point of view. What if such transmitters – planted by advanced extraterrestrial civilizations – already exist on Earth and have been growing under our very noses for millennia?

'I think this is the most interesting thing I've done with my life.'
MP Christopher Mayhew (TV interview)

It's 1955 and somewhere in the BBC's Broadcasting House in London, the avuncular, bespectacled **Dr Humphry Osmond** is administering 400 mg of mescaline to British MP Christopher Mayhew, who has agreed to take the psychoactive drug as an experiment for a BBC *Panorama* Special.

While respectably attired in suit and tie, once the drug has began to have effect, Mayhew visibly slouches back in his chair with a sloppy grin on his face. 'I am conscious that there is no absolute space or time,' he says, 'merely what we have constructed.' Reflecting afterwards on the experience he observed: 'I felt a state of euphoria that didn't last for minutes but months. I believe my experiences were real and took place outside of time. Psychiatrists may explain it away but they didn't have the experience.' Unfortunately the BBC also deemed his experiences invalid and the program was never broadcast.

Like the far reaches of the universe, the psychedelic realm really is unchartered terrain. Cinematic clichés of refracted lenses, distorted images, bad Jazz music and protracted wah-wah solos offer little insight into the other-worldly irrational nature of a 'trip'. Commonly reported experiences are intense colours, complex patterns and a sense of timelessness and unity with the universe. For the minority who experience a 'bad trip', it might be the worst experience of their lives, inducing paranoia, the screaming meemies and the terrifying sensation of dying. Strangest of all are alleged encounters with unearthly entities; psychedelic plants can open up a world inhabited by angels, aliens and creatures straight from the pages of a Tolkien novel. Author

As well as introducing Aldous Huxley to mescaline (which led to his writing *The Doors of Perception*, 1954), Dr Humphry Osmond was also responsible for coining the term 'psychedelics'. And yes the spelling of his name is correct, a true psychonaut he dropped an 'e'.

and psychedelic researcher Terence McKenna described the creatures he regularly saw on hallucinatory experiences as 'self-replicating machine elves'. To the myriad shamanic cultures across the globe, these entities are almost universally thought of sacred spirits whose intelligent is far greater than ours.

In pointing our radio telescopes into deep space, hoping for signals from extraterrestrials, is it possible that we've been looking in the wrong places all this time? Would superior life forms really use such crude methods of communication as radio waves? Instead, what if certain psychedelic substances are the dial to allow us to tune in to alien communications, transmitted via DNA? To further explore this outlandish idea we need to journey back a few decades when a new(ish) theory of the origin of life was being explored by the nobel prize-winning scientist, Francis Crick.

Francis Crick, a British molecular biologist, biophysicist and neuroscientist, most noted for being a co-discoverer of the structure of the DNA molecule in 1953.

THE ORIGINS OF DNA

In 1979, Crick's second book *Life Itself, Its Origin and Nature*, was published, championing a theory known as directed panspermia. Part of the team who had discovered DNA, Crick had come to the conclusion that the DNA molecule – the building block of all life – was just too complex to have emerged fully formed on this planet.

One of the many astounding properties of DNA is its capability as a recording device, leading it to be known as 'The Book of Life.' Far beyond the most advanced computer we can imagine, one DNA molecule is capable of storing the knowledge of an entire civilization. How could such a thing just pop into existence out of the primordial soup? The answer, for Crick, was that it couldn't. Instead, he reasoned that DNA had been deliberately shipped to our planet as a bacteria **by an alien life form more advanced than our own** but on the verge of collapse. Fans of the film *Prometheus* (2012) may be nodding their heads at this point. Anyone who has seen Ridley Scott's film cannot forget the opening sequence in which an alien humanoid is left on Earth to sacrifice itself to the greater good. It drinks some black goo and begins to dissolve into a waterfall. The message is clear – as its DNA mixes with our water this is how life began on Earth.

That life on Earth first originated from a more advanced alien culture may be a plausible theory but it still sidesteps the more fundamental question of how life began in the first place or if, indeed, the universe has ever been anything other than alive.

The scientific community remains divided as to whether water came to our planet via comets and asteroids but as a theory it is taken seriously. **That DNA may have got here by similar means also has growing support in the field of astrobiology**. Crick's notion that DNA was sent here by a dying civilization, however, seems an unnecessary complication in the theory so let's put it to one side. Besides, we need to keep things relatively simple to make room for the introduction of an equally bizarre molecule into the story: DMT.

One current theory suggests DNA could be carried through the universe by fungi; spores have been found to survive in deep space.

Chemical compound for dimethyltryptamine.

DMT, or N-N dimethyltryptamine, is a simple molecule common in nature and known to induce strong hallucinations in humans. It is found in hundreds of plants, fungi, some amphibians and a small number of fish. It is believed to be found in our pineal gland and

released during birth, death and dreaming, although this has yet to be
proven scientifically. Despite DMT's relative ubiquity, as yet its only
purpose appears to be to send us into altered states of consciousness.
And yet ritualistic use of 'sacred' psychedelic substances (many, but not
all of which, contain DMT) is common to every ancient culture that
had access to them. Tribes in the Americas use tobacco, mescaline
and ayahuasca; in Europe and Asia it's magic mushrooms and fly
agarics; Africa has cannabis and iboga, the Australian Aborigines
have acacia. And this is to name but a few; we'll save the drinking
of reindeer urine for another day. In Western culture, psychedelic
enthusiasts are most likely to explain their reason for taking them
as to 'expand consciousness', or 'explore altered states'. In traditional
cultures the response is different, they are not taken simply to spend
hours staring in wonder at the patterns in the carpet but to journey to
the underworld to connect with spirits. The questions is, why?

THE COSMIC SERPENT

One of the great enigmas of human evolution is how our ancestors acquired their medical knowledge. Received wisdom is that we figured stuff out by trial and error – you get haemorrhoids and so experiment with rubbing different leaves into the afflicted area until one of them relieves the pain. Not only can you sit down again without making involuntary moans, but you've also discovered the essential ingredients for Anusol. But not all anthropologists find trial and error a satisfying enough theory when it comes to compound medicines. Take curare;

DMT crystals.

an ancient poison used in blow-darts to render animals unconscious and now utilized by Western medicine. There are dozens of types of curare manufactured in the Amazon but making it is far from straightforward; it requires the combining of several plants which are boiled together. Those making it must be careful not to breathe the fumes at this stage; they are highly toxic. Once reduced to a paste, curare is harmless if swallowed; it is only effective if injected under the skin. If, as some believe, curare couldn't have been stumbled upon through trial and error, how might we have discovered it?

Jeremy Narby, anthropologist and author of *The Cosmic Serpent* (1998), spent many decades studying and living with ayahuasca tribes of the Amazon. In observing and working with ayahuasca shaman – or ayahuasqueros – Narby came to the conclusion that their psychedelic brew was taking users to a molecular level (the 'underworld') in which DNA was acting as transmitter for information passing

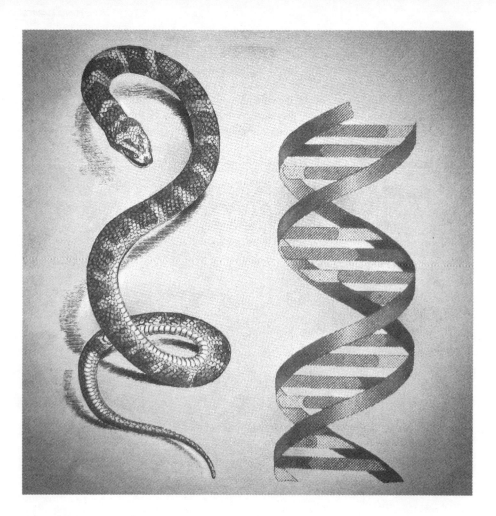

Stefan Gutemuth's
original artwork from
Jeremy Narby's book
The Cosmic Serpent,
alluding to the
similarities between
DNA and
ayahuasca-induced
snake paintings.

between the world of 'spirit' and human consciousness. It was as if
DMT turned users into living microscopes. For Narby, proof of the
pudding that traditional cultures had some understanding of DNA
was the common appearance in their art of entwined snakes, said
by shaman to symbolize 'secret knowledge'. These coiled serpents
looked so much like the classic double helix description of the DNA
molecule that Narby had to conclude that's exactly what they were.
If an experienced Amazonian shaman – or ayahuasquero – learned
how to communicate with the strange spirits encountered on DMT
they would impart secret knowledge, and DNA was the means to

enable two-way interactions with these other-worldly spirits. Whether Narby is correct or not, it is a curious factor that the inhabitants of the rainforest have never claimed that their medical knowledge came by trial and error; if an ayahuasquero is asked how he or she learned to paint or became expert in plant medicine, they really will reply, 'I was taught by spirits.'

Could it be that the rich cast of dwarves, fairies, elves, angels and trolls, who inhabit our fairy tales and myths, are a faint memory of these spirit creatures? Given that a unifying belief among all shamanic cultures is that the spirits of the underworld are real and hyper-intelligent, can we completely rule out the possibility these spirits might be a new starting point in our search for extraterrestrial life? While DNA can record the entire knowledge of a civilization, we remain a long way from understanding what this molecule is also capable of, or what really happens to our consciousness when we take DMT.

If you and everyone in your neighbourhood woke up one morning to discover you'd all had the same dream, what could you conclude from the experience? Mass delusion? Coincidence? You're trapped in an episode of *The Twilight Zone*? That different cultures across the globe have claimed, for millennia, to be communicating with unearthly creatures to gain secret knowledge should throw up similar questions. It might simply be our ancient cultures means of making sense of the world. Or maybe, just maybe, the entire human race has been hanging out with little green men since before recorded history. Whatever the case, isn't it time for Ridley Scott to make that movie? *DB*

SEEKERS' DIRECTORY

Operation Mindfuck

BOOKS *The Principia Discordia* (1963) is a Discordian religious text written by Greg Hill (Malaclypse the Younger) with Kerry Wendell Thornley (Lord Omar Khayyam Ravenhurst). This is the book that started it all. No need to buy a copy. Being copyright free, there are plenty of pdfs available online.

The Myth Gap: What Happens When Evidence and Arguments Aren't Enough (2017). Alex Evans argues that in this time of global crisis and transition – mass migration, inequality, resource scarcity and climate change – it is only by finding new myths, those that speak to us of renewal and restoration, that we will navigate our way to a better future.

The Cosmic Trigger trilogy (1997). Volume I charts Robert Anton Wilson's experiences putting himself through a process of 'self-induced brain change'.

PLAY *Cosmic Trigger* is a playful, four-hour, sex, drugs and psycho-drama, exploring the life of Robert Anton Wilson and his book *Cosmic Trigger*, written by Daisy Campbell (daughter of the late Ken Campbell). cosmictriggerplay.com

CREATE CHAOS Become an Ordained Minister in the Church of the subgenius subgenius.com. Dress up as Santa and maraud around your city: santacon.info

Tulpamancy

JOIN THE DISCUSSION Follow threads about Tulpas on reddit.com/r/Tulpas/ and tulpa.info

BOOK *Magic and Mystery In Tibet* (Alexandra David-Néel, 1932). Alexandra David-Néel was an occultist, anarchist and the most remarkable female travel writer of the twentieth century who immersed herself in Tibetan culture

and Buddhism. In 1914, she secluded herself in a cave in the Himalayas for two years, intensively studying the mysteries of Tibetan Buddhism and the mystic legends that surrounded Buddhist monks. The book records seemingly magic feats performed by Buddhist monks: telepathy, tumo breathing (the art of generating body heat to keep warm in freezing conditions); and the ability to run for days at a time, defy gravity and become invisible.

FILM *Unearthing* (Alan Moore, 2010) began as an essay published in Iain Sinclair's *London: City of Disappearances* in 2006. It was subsequently developed into a photographic book in collaboration with Mitch Jenkins and a filmed monologue. It explores the life and death of Alan Moore's friend Steve Moore, who created a moon goddess named Selene.

The men who scared themselves to death

BOOK *Sleep Paralysis: Night-mares, Nocebos, and the Mind Body Connection* (Professor Shelley Adler, 2011) delves into the phenomenon of sleep paralysis, calling on 15 years of field and archival research.

ART *The Nightmare* is a 1781 oil painting by Anglo-Swiss artist Henry Fuseli, portraying a sleeping woman with a demonic and ape-like incubus crouched on her chest. The painting influenced Mary Shelley in a scene from her famous Gothic novel *Frankenstein* (1818) and Edgar Allan Poe evoked *The Nightmare* in his short story 'The Fall of the House of Usher' (1839).

AUDIO *The Placebo Effect* (BBC Radio 4, 2004). In this two-part documentary, Ben Goldacre explores the effects of placebos and their implications for medicines:.

Man-size culture-bound syndromes

BOOK *Hikikomori: Adolescence without End* (Saito Tamaki, 2013). An English translation of the controversial Japanese bestseller that made the public aware of the social problem of *hikikomori*, which provoked a national debate about the causes and extent of the condition.

COMIC N.H.K. Tatsuhiko Takimoto is a Japanese author best known for his novel *Welcome to the N.H.K.* (2002), now a manga series with art by Kendi Oiwa. In the afterword for his novel, Takimoto wrote that he was a *hikikomori* and was still

recovering, revealing: 'the themes addressed in this story are not things of the past for me but currently active problems'. In a later edition, dated April 2005, he added that he was 'living as a parasite on the royalties from this book' and had since been 'completely unable to write'.

Roko's Basilisk

JOIN THE DISCUSSION Investigate thought experiments such as Roko's Basilisk, with other users at lesswrong.com, an online community dedicated to the study and improvement of human rationality.

(Illegal) encounters with aliens

FILM In the opening sequence of *Prometheus* (2012), an alien humanoid is left on Earth to sacrifice itself to the greater good. It drinks some black goo and begins to dissolve into a waterfall, thus planting the DNA that begins life on Earth.

DOCUMENTARY *DMT: The Spirit Molecule* (2010). An investigation into the mysteries of dimethyltryptamine (DMT), a molecule found in nearly every living organism and considered the most potent psychedelic on Earth.

The Mescaline Experiment with Christopher Mayhew is available on YouTube.

BOOKS Explore some of the big ideas around the nature and uses of psychedelics in *The Doors of Perception* (Aldous Huxley, 1954), *The Cosmic Serpent: DNA and the Origins of Knowledge* (Jeremy Narby, 1999) and *Life Itself: Its Origin and Nature* (Francis Crick, 1982).

the really creepy stuff

The detached human feet of the Salish Sea

A singular case for Sherlock

Ten years ago, something washed up on a beach in Jedediah Island, British Columbia, that was so mysterious and macabre it would have inspired a case worthy of the great consulting detective, Sherlock Holmes. Had he not been fictitious, Holmes would have been there like a shot, abandoning his opium-infused revelries to scour the beaches for clues, Watson close behind him, dreaming up a suitable title for their latest adventure.

It all began on 20 August, 2007 when a young girl holidaying in the area found a size 12 trainer on the ground. Intrigued, she picked it up, discovering to her horror that inside the frayed remnants of a sock lay a decomposing human foot. Six days later another right foot – also inside a size 12 trainer – was found on nearby Gabriola Island. By the following summer, a further four human feet had been found in the area and yet another on a beach in Washington State; all around the shorelines of the Strait of Georgia, which divides the two areas. Nearly all were right feet, sporting modern trainers or hiking boots. The first foot – via DNA testing – was eventually traced to a local man diagnosed with depression and believed to have drowned himself; it didn't, however, account for the others. Over the next few years, more feet followed, totalling ten in British Columbia and four in Washington State. As Holmes, with his dark humour, might have quipped: 'Watson, the game's afoot!'

At first, the sinister flotsam was believed to be the work of a serial killer, but forensic ruled this out; there was no sign of mutilation, the feet had **separated from the bodies naturally** through decomposition.

This, however, did not rule out the possibility that the bodies had been deliberately weighed down and dumped in the water. As one had been traced to a depressed man, could the rest also have been victims of suicide, throwing themselves off British Columbia's many bridges?

Hands and feet are the first to separate from a dead body in water, owing to wrists and ankles being vulnerable and weak areas.

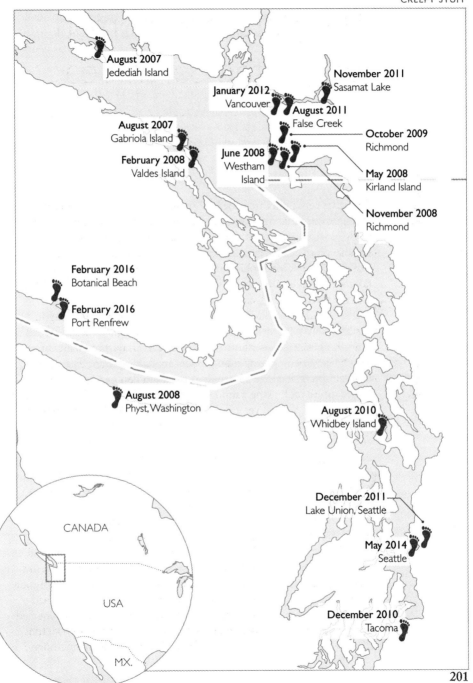

August 2007
Jedediah Island

November 2011
Sasamat Lake

January 2012
Vancouver

August 2011
False Creek

October 2009
Richmond

August 2007
Gabriola Island

June 2008
Westham
Island

May 2008
Kirland Island

February 2008
Valdes Island

November 2008
Richmond

February 2016
Botanical Beach

February 2016
Port Renfrew

August 2008
Physt, Washington

August 2010
Whidbey Island

December 2011
Lake Union, Seattle

May 2014
Seattle

December 2010
Tacoma

CANADA

USA

MX.

If this was the case, why had the feet only started appearing up after 2007? Some theorized that the feet might have belonged to victims of the 2004 Tsunami, but when several more were identified as being local, this too was ruled out.

It didn't help that by 2008 a number of hoax feet also began to be discovered on the beaches – one, a trainer containing a stuffed animal paw inside, another with raw meat inside a sock; others filled with chicken bones and the skeleton of a dog's foot.

All was quiet for a number of years until February 2016, when yet another disembodied foot was found on Botanical Beach in British Columbia. Five days later its pair appeared on nearby Port Renfrew.

Some – but not all – of the feet have since been traced to missing people. Speculation that added air pockets in modern trainers and hiking shoes could kept feet afloat for years before they are discovered might explain why other types of footwear have not been found. But as these types of footwear have been fashionable since the 90s, it still doesn't explain why disembodied feet hadn't been found before 2007. And finally, the odds of finding so many feet – not to mention complete pairs turning up – is so astronomical, that it seems unlikely this strange case will ever be fully solved. To this day, not a single footless body has ever been found.

Would Holmes have figured it out? Of course he would, doubtless solving the case in a matter hours, later remarking to Watson over his second pipe, 'I deduced the whole thing from the singular scuff marks on the inside sole of the size 11 walking boot.' DB

Petrified to death

Cryonics, cyborgs and self-mummification

It's 1970 and Raymond Martinot, a doctor teaching medicine in Paris, buys himself a château in the Pays de la Loire region of France. His ambition: to create a working space to pursue his interest in cryobiology and life extension. Within four years, Martinot has built himself a bespoke freezer, in which to store his own corpse, to be housed in the chateaux's vaulted cellar.

Fourteen years later, his wife Monique passes away from ovarian cancer. Grief-stricken, Martinot decides to preserve her body in the special freezer, initiating a two-decade legal battle with the French authorities to keep her there. Before the case is resolved, Martinot himself dies in 2002 from a fatal stroke. Dutifully his son, Remy, freezes his father's body and picks up the court case. Proceedings are cut short four years later when the freezer malfunctions, raising the temperature from −65 °C to −20 °C. The bodies of Remy's parents begin to thaw and he is forced to cremate their remains, bringing the 36-year cryonics experiment to an end.

The ethical, legal and practical quandaries surrounding life extension continue to this day. In 2016, a British court ruled that a dying 14-year-old girl should be allowed to have her body cryogenically preserved following her death from a rare form of cancer. Her poignant letter to the court implored: 'I don't want to be buried underground. I want to live and live longer and I think that in the future they might find a cure for my cancer and wake me up. I want to have this chance. This is my wish.' The girl, known only as JS, is now among the 200 bodies being preserved at −196°c in one of two high-tech laboratories in the US.

Our desire to pause, reverse or transcend our own mortality has tortured us for millennia: from ancient embalmers and the immortal fantasies of Ancient Greece to a generation where administering Botox and dedicating our lives to creative 'immortality projects' appears utterly normal. Arguably, it underpins many world religions. But is our desire for immortality merely wishful thinking or is the technology, born within the pages of science fiction, finally ready to let us cheat death?

Today's **experiments in life preservation** range from macabre to the mundane. Trials in cryonics are being played out in the high-tech laboratories of Arizona to the sheds of Sussex; internet entrepreneurs are investigating ways to download their brains onto virtual avatars so they can pursue their hobbies indefinitely; swathes of people are pursuing 'amortal' lives, living agelessly and denying the passage of time; that's before we even get started on the grisly act of self-mummification.

But other than the question of whether we can do it, might the question also be should we be doing this? Attempts to control our own mortality raise ethical, philosophical and legal conundrums and force us to confront the material or immaterial nature of our souls. What follows is not light reading, so a word of caution: pondering your own mortality, and ways to transcend it, can lead to what Douglas Adams called, 'The long, dark tea-time of the soul.'

CRYONICS AND THE PROSPECT OF IMMORTALITY

Like many scientific developments, cryonics – preserving cadavers in the hope that scientific advances might one day be able to restore them – was born within the pages of science fiction. In the 1930s, a young Robert Ettinger was absorbed in his copy of pulp fiction magazine *Amazing Stories* when he stumbled upon a story called 'The Jameson Satellite'. In the story, The Last Earthman, Professor Jameson, becomes obsessed with the idea of preserving his body and successfully launches his cadaver into space. Forty million years later it is found orbiting a dead planet Earth by passing Zoromes – cyborgs who've achieved immortality by transferring their organic brains to machine bodies – who revive the professor.

The story clearly left a deep impression on Ettinger. Later in life – and now a physics teacher – he wrote: 'It was instantly obvious to me that the author had missed the main point of his own idea! If immortality is achievable through the ministrations of advanced aliens through repairing a human corpse, then why should not everyone be frozen to await later rescue by our own people?' (Foreword to the 1987 printing of *The Prospect of Immortality*).

In 1948, Ettinger expanded on the idea in his seminal publication *The Prospect of Immortality* (1962). His aim was to inspire people to make the fiction a reality. The cryonics movement – or as he called it, 'The Freezer-Centered Era' – has been ticking along under the radar ever since.

Robert Ettinger
was inspired to
explore cryonics
thanks to this 1931
edition of *Amazing
Stories* containing
a story called The
Jameson Satellite.

In 2006, British photographer Murray Ballard embarked on a
ten-year project to investigate the practice Ettinger inspired. His
photographs document the small but dedicated international cryonics
community, lifting the lid on a practice that is both futuristic and
surprisingly rudimentary. 'Ettinger thought cryonics would be a huge
global industry and that every town and city would have a cryonics
facility by now,' Ballard told us. 'Instead, there are only three official
cryonic facilities: two in the US and one in Russia.'

Performing its first human cryopreservation on 16 July 1976, Alcor Life Extension Foundation in Arizona has since stored over 150 bodies in liquid nitrogen; a further 1,128 members are signed up for being cryogenically preserved after death. In each case, the Alcor team will rush to the patient's bedside as the end draws near then, 60–120 seconds after death is pronounced, will commence the correct cryonic procedures. This involves: rapidly cooling the donor's body; restoring oxygenation and circulation using an automated heart-lung; preserving vital organs; draining the blood and replacing it with vitrifying agents – medical-grade anti-freeze to keep cells intact – then hanging the body upside down in a sleeping bag. Patients are then shipped to Alcor to be stored in what looks like giant thermos flasks.

It sounds like they've got things in hand but bear in mind, if you don't happen to live close to one of the world's three cryonics facilities, this all needs to be done with a portable 'perfusion kit'. In Britain, you can sign up to a standby service. For £27,870, Cryonics UK will rock up in their specially-designed ambulance and prepare your body for shipping. You can't get a banana through US customs, but there's no prohibition in place for posting human remains, apparently, provided the correct procedures are in place.

The FAQ on the Cryonics, UK website puts this in a rather more straightforward manner: 'Q: How can I tell that it works? A: You can't. You have a choice, though: you can try it, and maybe live and maybe die. Or you can not try it, and definitely die.'

With people putting so much time and money into the procedure, it begs the question: **does it actually work**? The truth is, nobody knows. Even Alcor admits the technology is still a work in progress: 'No adult human has ever been revived from temperatures far below freezing. Cryonics patients are cared for in the expectation that future technology, especially molecular nanotechnology, will be available to reverse damage associated with the cryonics process.'

Cryopreservation is now an established process. Human embryos can survive at −196 °C for ten years under well-controlled laboratory conditions. In 2016, scientists successfully reanimated a rabbit's brain, so why not a whole human?

The freezing part isn't proving too much trouble, but what about thawing? We're assuming it's not going to be as easy as plunging the patient into 'warm liquid goo' and then letting them go for a very long wee, à la Austin Powers. Frogs in subarctic Alaska can survive at −14°C by producing their own cryoprotectants, substances that lower the body's freezing point and prevent the ice from forming within their cells. Humans, on the other hand, don't produce their own anti-freeze (yet) and are ill-designed to being frozen and defrosted; when our cells freeze, they fill with ice crystals, expanding and rupturing the cell walls. Surely this is a recipe for mushy brains.

Standby team training,
Sheffield, South Yorkshire,
July 2010 (Murray Ballard).

Cryostats – apparatus
used to maintain
constant low
temperature – at the
Cryonics Institute,
Michigan, April 2010.
Six patients are
stored in each one.
(Murray Ballard).

207

Patient storage
demonstration,
Alcor Life Extension
Foundation,
Scottsdale, Arizona.
August 2009
(Murray Ballard)

WORTH THE RISK?

Ettinger once said, 'The likely prize [of cryonics being feasible]
is so enormous that even slender odds would be worth embracing.'
He died, or rather 'completed his first lifecycle', in 2011 at the age
of 92. He is now stored at the Cryonics Institute in Michigan,
where he became their 106th patient. Speaking to Ballard before his

death, Ettinger spoke about how difficult it is to shift mainstream thinking and patterns of behaviour, and how he'd underestimated that people are inherently cautious and conservative. But perhaps it pays to be cautious? Like Ettinger, you might think it's a no-brainer (excuse the pun); after all, the worst that could happen is that you'll stay dead, right? But is that strictly true? If cryonics proves fruitful in the future **it's worth considering who you would be waking up next to.** Currently, 75 per cent of the people stored at Alcor are men; many, we speculate, are elderly, ridiculously rich, have died from a terminal illness and believe vehemently in the sanctity of life. Oh and Simon Cowell recently let slip that he intends to have his corpse cryogenically frozen. Perhaps wait it out a few more years before signing up for that portable 'perfusion kit'?

DOWNLOADING YOUR BRAIN: THE 2045 INITIATIVE

If the case of Ettinger and cryonics is anything to go by, where else are we going to find our future realities but in science fiction? One recurrent idea is the 'brain in a jar', explored through a future version of Lister in *Red Dwarf*, Steve Martin in *The Man With Two Brains* (1983) and the entire premise of the *Matrix* series.

Could the contents of our brains one day be downloaded to a computer, ready to be re-uploaded to another available brain or even to pilot a non-organic host body?

This thought experiment has been picked up by Dmitry Itskov, a Russian billionaire and internet entrepreneur frustrated that he can't pursue all of his hobbies to a point of mastery within his lifetime. To this end, he founded the 2045 Initiative, 'to create technologies enabling the transfer of an individual's personality to a more advanced non-biological carrier, and extending life, including to the point of immortality'.

Itskov intends to make this possible by 2045, but the timeline on his website seems to be a touch hasty. By 2015–2020, he expects: 'The emergence and widespread use of affordable android 'avatars' controlled by a 'brain-computer' interface.' By 2020, we'll see the 'creation of an autonomous life-support system for the human brain linked to a robot' and in 2035, we'll be able to transfer consciousness onto an artificial carrier. By 2045, our 'substance-independent minds' will receive new bodies together with capacities far exceeding those of ordinary humans. 'A new era for humanity will arrive!'

Of course, not only do the timescales seem a little optimistic the real spanner in Itskov's works is that science still has little to no

In Woody Allen's *Sleeper* (1973), Miles Monroe wakes from a routine operation in the early 1970s to find himself hundreds of years in the future. He is given chocolate cake and cigarettes to revive him. In the future, he discovers, they have been found to be the healthiest things known to humans.

In 1925, Soviet scientist Sergei Brukhonenko researched blood transfusions and developed the 'autojektor', one of the first heart and lung machines. He tested the success of these machines on decapitated dogs' heads. These experiments were recorded in the 1940 film *Experiments in the Revival of Organisms*, which show a dog's head eating sweets and licking its snout, attached to a pump. This state of 'life' was claimed to last for hours but actually only lasted a few minutes. Nonetheless, it was a major development in artificial life support and the development of cyborg technologies.

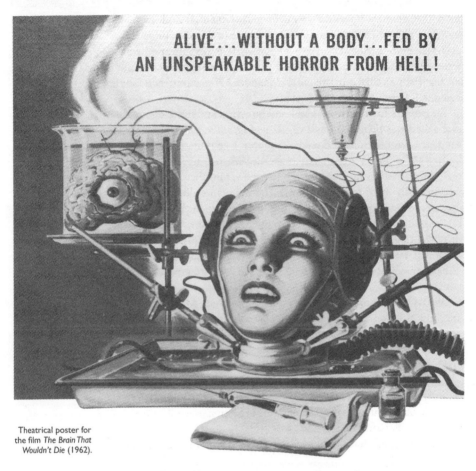

ALIVE...WITHOUT A BODY...FED BY
AN UNSPEAKABLE HORROR FROM HELL!

Theatrical poster for
the film *The Brain That
Wouldn't Die* (1962).

understanding of how consciousness works or where memory is
stored, never mind trying to fish it out of your brain with a spoon
and popping it onto a memory stick. We wish him luck.

SELF-MUMMIFICATION

Unlike many cultures that focused preservation on the elite, between
5050–1800 BC, the Chinchorro people of Chile mummified all of
their dead, from elders to miscarried foetuses. Embalmers replaced
soft tissues with botanical fibres and animal hair, reinforced bones
with sticks, stripped back the skin, smoothed the corpse with clay or
fish glue, wrapped it in reeds and left it to dry out for 30–40 days.

You might find the idea of being mummified rather grisly, but

more disturbing still was the practice of *sokushinbutsu*: Buddhist
monks abiding by asceticism (a strict lifestyle of self-discipline and
abstinence) to the point of death and entering mummification while
alive. And yes, you read that right. The practice, which came to light
in the 1960s, occurred between the 11th and 19th centuries in China,
India and Japan.

The process took between eight and ten years and involved a strict
diet called *mokujikigyo* (translating as 'eating a tree'). The monks would
eat pine needles, resins and seeds – thought to eliminate fat in the
body – and reduce water intake to shrink their organs. Towards the
end, they would drink a poisonous tea made from the sap of the urushi
tree, normally used to lacquer bowls. The monks would then position
themselves inside a stone tomb not much larger than their meagre
bodies, with a tube through which to breathe, and meditate until they
died in a state of *jhana* (meditation), their bodies naturally preserved.
Each day they would ring a bell to let others know they were alive.
When the bell stopped ringing, the tube would be removed and the
tomb sealed.

Twenty-four mummies have been found in Japan so far; the rest
are thought to be buried beneath the sacred mountains of Haguro,
Gassan and Yudono in modern-day Yamagata Prefecture. The monks
didn't see the practice as suicide, rather a step towards spiritual
enlightenment.

While self-embalming is, fortunately, a thing of the past (the most
recently-discovered *sokushinbutsu* mummy is 200 years old), there
are still communities that practice mummification – albeit in the
traditional way, after death.

In 1975, Claude 'Corky' Nowell – a 30-year-old American graphics

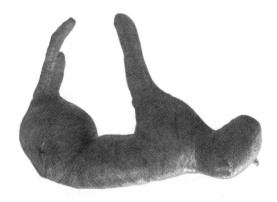

Mummified cat by
Summum in Utah.

211

Summum pyramid in Utah

salesman – was trying to relax after a busy day when he was visited by a number of hairless, blue beings. These 'Summa Individuals' took him to their pyramid and let him in on some truths about the nature of creation – concepts, they said, have always existed but they have to continually re-introduce to humankind.

To spread the message, Nowell – now known as Corky Ra – founded Summum, a religion and philosophy that draws on both ancient Egyptian practices and the Hebrew prophet Moses together with **winemaking** and sexual ecstasy.

Followers practice mummification as a means of guiding one's essence to a greater destination. The process takes 90 days: the organs are removed; the corpse is submerged in a 'baptismal font' of 'secret formula' chemicals; it is then covered in lanolin and wax, and wrapped in cotton gauze with a fancy fibre-glass finish; as a finishing touch, the body is encased in a bronze casket. The first person to receive this elaborate treatment was Corky Ra himself, following his death in 2008. His body is now housed within the group's 26-foot pyramid, which stands in an industrial compound just off an interstate in Salt Lake City, Utah.

Today, Summum offers the world's only modern mummification service. They mainly do pets – cats, peacocks and even finches have undergone the ritual – paid for by generous donations. *JK & GL*

212

The death of Elisa Lam

The internet's creepiest CCTV footage

On 13 February 2013, LA police released CCTV footage of a missing girl, Elisa Lam. Lam – a 21-year-old student from Canada on a solo tour of the West Coast – had been missing for two weeks. After checking into the Cecil Hotel on 26 January, she hadn't been seen or heard from since the 31st. Her last known whereabouts were from footage recorded in the hotel elevator, captured on the day she disappeared.

The footage was so bizarre that when it was released on the internet, it went viral. Things get creepy from the moment Lam steps into the lift. The door doesn't close and appears to be faulty. Lam waits, then pokes her head out of the lift, glancing suspiciously down the corridor, as if someone is following her. She then rushes back in and stands with her back to the control panel, appearing to hide from someone or something. The girl then proceeds to press all the buttons but the lift door still refuses to close. She exits and re-enters the lift, again glancing around, and makes little hopping movements around the lift as if playing a game. At one point she returns to the corridor, her hands outstretched and raised, fingers spliced, as if she is swimming in the air. Other times she disappears almost completely.

The young girl's behaviour is so erratic that she gives the appearance of a woman possessed. After four minutes, she finally vacates the lift and the doors close, only to open twice more, each time to reveal an empty corridor.

Six days after the footage was released, a guest complained to hotel staff that the water in his room was coming out black and foul smelling. The caretaker went up to the roof and discovered the cause: the naked, drowned body of Elisa Lam, face up inside one of the hotel's four water towers, her clothes floating beside her. She had drowned only hours after exiting the lift.

The autopsy showed no signs of foul play, nor evidence to suggest suicide, and so the police cited accidental death as the cause of Lam's demise. Her medical notes revealed that Lam had been diagnosed with depression and bipolar disorder. Lam had, they surmised, undressed, climbed into the water tank and drowned.

But it didn't quite add up. Lam's mobile phone was never found and her Tumblr account continued to be updated for several weeks after her death. Her body was reported as being covered in a mysterious sandy substance. And the hotel staff were baffled as to how Lam gained access to the roof of the hotel in the first place, without setting off its door alarms.

Water tanks on the roof of the infamous Cecil Hotel.

After a few days at the hotel, her roommates had complained about Lam's 'odd behaviour' and she had been relocated from a dorm to a single room. There was, however, nothing in her blog to suggest she was contemplating suicide; residents of the hotel and a local bookshop owner had all described her as being in good spirits on the day that she drowned. Some speculated that Lam's erratic behaviour in the lift implied she was on hallucinogens, but the toxicologist's report showed she was clean.

For believers of the paranormal, things get a little odder from this point on. Lam's tragic story closely parallels the plot of the 2002 horror film *Dark Water*, in which a young girl drowns after falling into a water tank in a run-down building with a malfunctioning lift. The weirdness doesn't stop there. Over the years, the Cecil Hotel – known by some, distastefully, as 'the suicide hotel' – has struggled to shake off a seedy and sinister reputation. Starting life as an upmarket hotel in the twenties, it hit the skids during the recession and never recovered, opening its doors to vulnerable and, on occasion, unsavoury characters. Numerous guests have jumped to their deaths over the years, one killing a passing pedestrian. Between 1984–1985, the Cecil was also home to serial killer, Richard 'the Night Stalker' Ramirez, a satanist who murdered 13 people. A few years later, serial killer, Jack Unterweger, who strangled prostitutes, stayed there too. In the CCTV footage, Lam appears to be either hiding from or perhaps talking to someone. This, combined with the hotel's tragic history, has led some to conclude that, like Jack Torrance in *The Shining*, Elisa Lam had been possessed by one of the spirits that haunted the building.

Considering Lam's medical history, her behaviour may have been due to a psychotic episode. Other theories emerged to suggest that Lam's erratic manner was caused by her being delirious with tuberculosis. A virulent outbreak of TB had affected thousands of people in LA at the time, with many cases in neighbourhoods surrounding The Cecil Hotel. As if it really couldn't get any weirder, the test for diagnosing tuberculosis is known as LAM-ELISA.

While rebranded at the end of 2013 as the boutique Stay on Main (it's located on Main Street), a city ordinance required that the hotel should keep half of its rooms for low-income tenants. It is now split into two halves – one aimed at international travellers like Lam, with a movie lounge and Xbox games, the other to cater for long-term lodgers. They have separate entrances, but share the elevator.

Although the CCTV footage is creepy to watch and it's curious to explore how a mystery unfolds on the internet, it's worth remembering that at the heart of this enigma is the death of a vulnerable young woman. Lam's Tumblr account – Nouvelle Nouveau – is still active, full of images from the worlds of fashion literature and art together with musings on anxiety and depression and quotes that inspired her. It's a poignant reminder of the unfolding passions of a woman at the beginning of her life. Nouvelle Nouveau begins with a quote from Chuck Palahniuk, 'You're always haunted by the idea you're wasting your life.' Not only was Lam denied a long life in which to reflect back on how well she spent it, it seems unlikely that we'll never know the circumstances which led to her tragic death. DB

HOW TO PLAY: ELEVATOR TO THE OTHER WORLD

While many of the theories attempting to explain Lam's death verge on the supernatural, perhaps the strangest one is that she was attempting to play an obscure Korean game which, if its instructions are correctly followed, purports to take the player to another world from which they might never return. This 'Other World' is said to be similar to our own with two key differences: it is much darker and the player of the game is its sole occupant.

Anyone wishing to play Elevator to the Other World, please note, this is a game for one player and can only be done in a building over ten storey's high. The writers of this book accept no responsibility for what might happen as a consequence.

INSTRUCTIONS:

01 Enter the lift on the first floor, alone, and head to the fourth. (If anyone enters the lift you must wait for them to leave and begin again on the first floor.)

02 Do not get out; remain in the elevator and press the button for the second floor.

03 Do not get out; remain in the elevator and press the button for the sixth floor.

04 Do not get out; remain in the elevator and head for the tenth floor. If you hear a voice calling you, do not answer.

05 Do not get out; remain in the elevator and return to the fifth floor. If a strange woman enters do not acknowledge her in any way. Avoid eye contact.

06 Do not get out; remain in the elevator and press the button for the first floor. If the lift begins heading to the first floor, get off immediately; something has gone wrong. If you have performed the ritual correctly you will instead find yourself heading to the tenth floor. If the woman asks where you are going or begins screaming, ignore her and show no fear.

07 At the tenth floor, if you have the courage, leave the elevator and enter the Other World. You will know it is the otherworld as you will be the sole occupant of the new land. It will be the one you just left only darker. And you will be the sole occupant. You may see a red cross in the distance. Any mobile devices will prove to be inoperable.

08 Should you look directly at the woman during any of the initial ritual of the game, the rules are very clear: she will keep you for her own.

09 Sweet dreams.

Gloria Ramirez

The Toxic Lady

In the 'Erlenmeyer Flask' – the 24th episode of *The X-Files* – special agents Mulder and Scully uncover a secret government experiment concerning alien DNA in which one of the research subjects escapes from an ambulance, his body having emitted a noxious gas which renders the onboard medics unconscious.

No, not simply a result of one too many vindaloos, or an embarrassing inability to process pulses; it's all explained away by aliens and underhand government activities. However, the notion of a toxic gas escaping from a human being and wreaking havoc was not an original one; it really happened – and, as so often is the case, the true explanation is even stranger than fiction.

In February 1994, when Gloria Ramirez was rushed into the emergency room at Riverside General Hospital in California with cardiac and respiratory difficulties, the only thing on the minds of the medical staff was to stabilize her.

Sadly, it was not to be. The 31-year-old, diagnosed with cervical cancer only a few weeks earlier, soon went into cardiac arrest and was pronounced dead within an hour of being admitted. But this was not the only incident that occurred during that hour – the events that followed her initial admittance continue to be the subject of debate and scientific discussion. Gloria Ramirez seems, unknowingly, to have infected over 50 per cent of the emergency room staff – but with what? No one knew.

When Gloria arrived at the ER, her breathing was shallow and her heart was beating rapidly – she was conscious but barely responding to questions. Drugs were administered to sedate her and normalize her heartbeat. Maureen Welch, the respiratory therapist on duty that night, attempted to resuscitate her, but it soon became apparent that staff would have to defibrillate her heart. As they placed electrodes on her chest, several staff noticed an oily sheen covering Gloria's body. Not only that; some also smelled a garlicky odour that they assumed was coming from her mouth. Susan Kane, a nurse who was collecting blood from her arm, noticed a 'foul' smell as she filled the syringe, and saw manila-coloured particles floating in the vial.

Much later, Welch would note that the blood smelled like ammonia, which surprised her not least because she had expected, if anything, 'a putrid smell' often associated with those receiving chemotherapy. Why 'much later'? Because Maureen Welch was incapacitated – as were several others. A matter of minutes after Ramirez's blood was taken, Susan Kane collapsed in the emergency room, medical resident Julie Gorchynski fainted at the nurse's desk, and Welch followed suit shortly afterwards. Other staff members started to complain of feeling ill, too.

Symptoms ranged from queasiness to burning sensations on the skin. Some suffered from apnoea – a temporary suspension of breathing – and others experienced tremors and uncontrolled limb movements. Of all those affected, Gorchynski's symptoms were the most severe: as well as interrupted breathing, hepatitis and pancreatitis, she also experienced avascular necrosis of the knees (essentially a kind of gangrene that affects the bones – treatable but very unpleasant and not what you would expect as a work-related illness, unless you're in the nerve-gas industry). Out of 37 emergency room staff that night, 23 reported at least one symptom and five were hospitalized.

NOT A SINGLE CLUE

The hospital administrators declared an internal emergency – all ER patients were evacuated to the car park. In case the situation transpired to stem from a chemical spill or escaped gas, those staff members who had experienced unpleasant symptoms were stripped to their underwear and had their clothes sealed in plastic bags. As staff and patients alike were treated under the car park lights, everyone waited for the hazard team to arrive and start their investigation.

Organophosphates were among the first chemical culprits to be considered; the symptoms exhibited by the staff seemed to fit, and yet the hazardous materials team found no evidence in the emergency room of either phosgene (which can rip open lung capillaries, drowning a victim in their own blood) or sewer gas (hydrogen sulphide that can kill a person with one whiff). And besides, why would these killers be present at Riverside Hospital in the first place?

The next step was to collect samples from the body of Gloria Ramirez, now lying in a sealed chamber – and this is where the

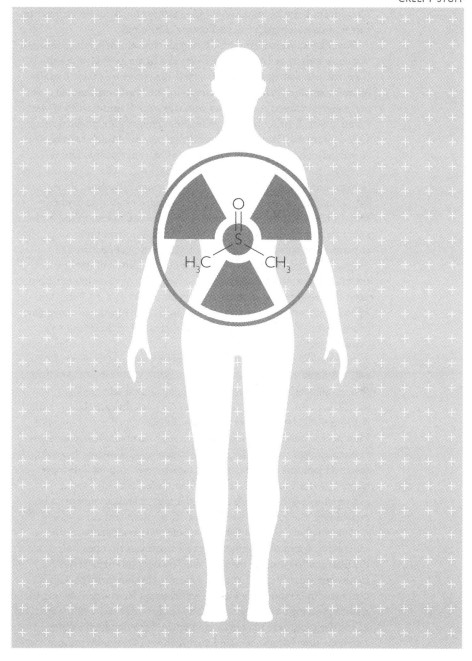

mystery deepens, because the coroner's office found nothing. Twenty-three 'victims', a dead body and not a single clue?

The samples were sent to the forensic science centre at Livermore National Laboratory, where Dr Brian Andresen took up the case. Each sample was analysed and any gas that had potentially leaked into the top of each container was also vented off and checked – but no gas (other than the kind one would expect to find in a body) was noted. More detailed tests identified specific compounds floating around Ramirez's system; all were drugs one would expect to find in someone fighting cancer. But then a few slightly odd elements emerged: nicotinamide, amine and large amounts of dimethyl sulfone (a compound sometimes produced in our bodies from sulphur-containing amino acids). The latter was the strangest thing in her system. However, that could easily be explained by her unhealthy liver being unable to break it down. The health department released its final conclusion in the September of that year. Ramirez had died of 'cardiac dysrhythmia caused by kidney failure as a result of her cervical cancer', they said. And why did the hospital staff become ill en masse? It was a simple a case of mass hysteria.

Predictably, those staff members – particularly the ones who had gangrenous knees – took great umbrage at having their symptoms brushed under the psychosomatic carpet. Welch approached Andresen again to ask him to have another look. This time she presented him with a scrapbook of notes, toxicology and coroner's reports she had been collecting since the incident.

A ONE-WOMAN NERVE-GAS FACTORY
Finally, in November 1994, Andresen and his deputy director, Patrick Grant, released their findings. They hypothesized that an extraordinary set of circumstances had turned Gloria Ramirez into a one-woman nerve-gas factory. The offending compound was DMSO – or dimethyl sulfoxide – and here's the journey it took to make so many people sick.

Gloria Ramirez rubs a DMSO cream on her skin (this is a home remedy used to reduce muscle and arthritic pain). In the ambulance, the paramedics give her oxygen, which combines with the DMSO in her system to create dimethyl sulfone – the relatively harmless chemical found during her autopsy. As Susan Kane draws blood, the dimethyl sulfone cools to room temperature to become supersaturated, hence the particles in the syringe. Some of the dimethyl sulfone breaks down in Ramirez's blood and some of those constituent parts combine with sulphates (common in the body) to make dimethyl sulphate which, on being released from Gloria's body through the syringe, escaped into the air.

And the indications of highly dimethyl sulphate – tested but never used as a war gas – was almost every symptom that was experienced in the ER that night.

Even though dimethyl sulphate doesn't vaporize easily, a small percentage of it will still evaporate at room temperature. It would take a lot of DMSO to start the process, but Andresen and Grant thought it perfectly conceivable that someone in the late stages of cancer might throw a lot at their body in an effort to give themselves a fighting chance. The coroner's report also showed Gloria to have a urinary blockage, meaning that if she was using DMSO a lot, it would have built up in her system. And finally, DMSO has a garlicky odour and leaves – yes, you've guessed it – an oily sheen on your skin.

The end, you might think. But Ramirez's family lawyer argued that she never used DMSO, while many scientists have pointed out that dimethyl sulphate's main symptom is eye irritation (not noted in any of the Riverside cases) and that most effects take several hours to act. Nevertheless, this explanation, endorsed by the coroner's office, continues to be the most scientifically feasible.

We may never know the truth behind this – one of the most wide-ranging forensic investigations ever undertaken – but the scientific team think medics should be wary: it may be rare, but one day we could see another unexpected chemical reaction in the ER, but until that day, Gloria Ramirez remains famously: The Toxic Lady. JT

MODERN-DAY END OF THE WORLD PROPHECIES

The end of the world used to be the sole province of visionaries, lunatics and cultists. Since the threat of climate change and the War on Terror, however, the apocalypse has been back in vogue, re-packaged by Hollywood in such epics as *The Day After* (1983), *The Last Wave* (1977) and *The Road* (2009). But while end of the world narratives about global warming or full-scale nuclear war remain a very real threat, in recent years more surreal and disturbing apocalyptic narratives have also come to the fore.

While preppers stock-pile automatic weapons and tinned peaches, and the super-rich build luxury apartments in hidden compounds, the stinking rich (think Silicon Valley whiz-kid billionaires) have been acquiring citizenships in supposedly safer states like New Zealand. Some of these same billionaires, perhaps signalling their disenchantment with our more prosaic apocalypses, have also become obsessed with the weirder disaster scenarios on offer, ideas that emerge from within the bowels of the internet in the minds of popular philosophers and AI experts.

Paypal billionaires Peter Thiel and Elon Musk have both funded efforts to envision possible threats to humanity from Artificial Intelligence. Their court philosopher is Nick Bostrom, a Swedish philosopher based at Oxford University, whose 2014 collection of apocalyptic thought-experiments *Superintelligence* was a surprise bestseller.

The Great Filter

The Great Filter is a horror story, invented by Swedish philosopher Nick Bostrom, concerning dead alien civilizations and deriving from the Fermi Paradox. This paradox results from the collision of two facts: there are billions of galaxies and planets, yet no convincing proof of extraterrestrial intelligence. Statistically, some of these planets would have to be fertile ground for the development of intelligent life.

The Great Filter seeks to resolve this paradox in the most spectacular and hideous way possible. Rather than suggest that other intelligent beings may not wish to leave their solar systems or – having observed our homicidal tendencies – prefer to stay hidden, the Great Filter presupposes that whenever a civilization reaches a certain threshold, some apocalyptic event extinguishes it. Exactly what this extinguishing event entails is unknown. Robin Hanson, who coined the term, argues that there must be a single common cause, writing, 'There thus exists a great filter between death and expanding lasting life. Humanity faces the ominous question: how far along this filter are we?'

Our only hope is the possibility that one of the earlier stages is the dangerous one, and we have passed through as a fluke. Thus, any discovery of extraterrestrial life on a lower scale than us would suggest the apocalypse occurs further up the timeline, which is seriously bad news for humanity.

As the philosopher Nick Land pessimistically observes, 'A galaxy teeming with life is a horror story. The less there is obstructing our being born, the more there is waiting to kill or ruin us.'

Extinction by self-replicating AI

The vogue for uncanny, humanoid robots seems to be currently at a low ebb (except, possibly, for sexbots). But, after lying fallow for 40-odd years, neural networking is having some great successes in so-called soft AI, such as beating human Go players and recognizing cat pictures on the internet. Neural networking attempts to mimic the non-hierarchical nature of human brain chemistry, thus potentially paving the way for AIs whose minds function in a similar fashion to their human counterparts. Despite humanity's penchant for creative self-destruction, the end of the world fear is not that our robot overlords might engage in some kind of Freudian revenge drama, but rather that they will *accidentally* eradicate us.

It will be far easier to create an AI with simple goals, such as to count the grains of sand on a beach or to maximize the total number of paperclips. The problem here is that creators will be more interested in getting AI to work rather than how, exactly, they will go about its business and whether the 'off' button will work. A sufficiently powerful, self-reinforcing AI whose only end is to maximize paperclip production may unceasingly continue its task until it has converted first the Earth and then increasingly large chunks of the observable universe into paperclips. The result? A surreal yet banal end of the world scenario straight from the pages of a Kurt Vonnegut novel.

Planetary mind theory

Our final end of the world scenario is so plausible that it just might be the most terrifying of all. It goes like this: as the world's technologies get ever more complex and biology and nanotechnology merge, the collective human race will eventually form a strange hybrid called a 'Planetary Mind', with all of us connected not just through social media but embedded microchips within our bodies, rendering us interdependent with digital technology.
The reality of a neuro-connected future is a realistic one; the question is: what happens if we all get infected with a nasty computer virus? Could one accidental piece of rogue coding wipe us all out? Or, is it more likely to be a deliberate act of sabotage on a global level? It might only need one disenfranchised bedroom geek with sufficient hacking skills to shut down the whole human race.
With this in mind, could the absence of any other life in the universe – The Great Filter – actually be the result of advanced nihilistic teenage aliens fed up with being 'misunderstood' and instigating an apocalypse just to annoy their parents? As the great Alan Partridge was want to say, 'And on that bombshell…' BB

SEEKERS' DIRECTORY

Detached human feet of the Salish Sea

COMEDY /TV If you need some lighthearted relief after this chapter, seek out detached foot-related comedy-horror programmes such as 'The Voodoo Feet of Death' from BBC's *Dr Terrible's House of the Horrible*, which stars Steve Coogan as a dancer who has his feet transplanted after an accident with a giant pair of scissors only to discover they once belonged to a murderer.

SHORT STORY *Sherlock Holmes: The Adventure of the Devil's Foot* (Sir Arthur Conan Doyle, 1910). Holmes and Watson investigate a case in which a sister is found dead and her two brothers, laughing hysterically in the same room, pronounced insane.

Petrified to death

BOOKS In 1962, Robert Ettinger published *The Prospect of Immortality*, the book that gave birth to the idea of cryonics, in which he sets out his ideas around the process of freezing a human body after death in the hope that scientific advances might one day restore life. All those active in cryonics today can trace their involvement, directly or indirectly, to the publication of Ettinger's books. Incidentally, Ettinger is now cryogenically preserved alongside his mother and his first and second wife. If we ever do figure out how to bring people back to life, that's going to be awkward.

Half a century later, between 2006 and 2015, Murray Ballard has undertaken an extensive photographic investigation of the practice Ettinger inspired, journeying through the small but dedicated international cryonics community, from the English seaside retirement town of Peacehaven; through the high-tech laboratories of Arizona; to the rudimentary facilities of KrioRus, on the outskirts of Moscow. Ballard's book *The Prospect of Immortality* (2016) is a fascinating insight into these worlds: gostbooks.com

FILMS Our obsession with cryonics continues to play out in science fiction: in Woody Allen's *Sleeper* (1973) a jazz musician and owner of the 'Happy Carrot' health-food store wakes from a routine operation in the early 1970s to find himself hundreds of years in the future, in a world where chocolate cake and cigarettes are said to be the healthiest things known to humans. *Forever Young* (1992) follows a World War Two test pilot who puts his head down for a year's hibernating in 1939 but ends up waking in the 90s. *Passengers* (2016) explores what happens when you wake 90 years too soon in deep space, with only an android bartender for company.

PRESERVE YOURSELF Sign up to be frozen and stored at the Alcor Life Extension Foundation in Arizona ($200,000 for the whole body, $80,000 for just your brain: alcor.org) If you live in Britain, for around £28,000, Cryonics UK will administer the initial medications following death, perfuse the head with cryo-protectant and ensure the body is shipped to the chosen cryonics storage provider: cryonics-uk.org

Summum can arrange for your body to be mummified after death, for a $67,000 donation, plus the cost of your burial casket: summum.org

The death of Elisa Lam

FILM *Dark Water* (2005) is a remake of a 2002 Japanese film by the same name, in which a young girl drowns after falling into a water tank in a run-down building with a malfunctioning lift.

Gloria Ramirez

TELEVISION *The X-Files: The Erlenmeyer Flask* (1994) features a character who emits a toxic gas when the paramedics perform a needle decompression in an ambulance. Is he infected with an extraterrestrial virus or did the man just have an overt fondness for pickled eggs?

Modern-day end of the world prophecies

FILMS Some alternative end of the world scenarios you might want to lose sleep over: Lars Von Trier's *Melancholia* (2011) is a haunting exploration of a dysfunctional family's final days as a rogue planet is set to collide with Earth, examining the human psyche in the face of disaster. *The Road* (2009) follows father and son as they struggle to survive after a global cataclysm has caused an extinction event. In *Take Shelter* (2011), a young father is plagued by apocalyptic visions and begins to build a shelter for his family in the back garden. His increasingly erratic behaviour leads others to question his sanity – is he a modern-day prophet or has he become lost in his delusions?

We don't recommend watching these films back to back. However, if you do splurge on dystopia, try one of these post-apocalyptic comedies as a 'palate-cleanser': *Shaun of the Dead* (2004), *Dr Strangelove* (1964) and *The Bed Sitting Room* (1969).

ACTIVITY Build your own post-apocalyptic compound in the garden using corrugated iron, MDF, a suitcase full of beans and a large dollop of misplaced optimism.

about the authors

DAVID BRAMWELL

David co-presents the fortnightly *Odditorium* podcast and presents and produces the *Waterfront* podcast on behalf of the Canal & River Trust. He is a regular contributor to BBC Radio 3 and Radio 4, has made programmes on Ivor Cutler and Damanhur for *Archive Hour* and *Between the Ears*, and been a guest on *The Museum of Curiosity* and *The Verb*. In 2011, he won a Sony Silver Award for his work on Radio 3's *The Haunted Moustache*.

He is the creator of the bestselling *Cheeky Guides* and author of two memoirs, *The No9 Bus to Utopia* (2014), ('Packed with gags, wisdom and pathos' – Tom Hodgkinson) and *The Haunted Moustache* (2016) ('Neurologically, this will light you up like a Christmas tree' – Alan Moore).

David has toured several award-winning shows and is the co-creator of Sing-along-a-Wickerman. He also gives entertaining lectures on topics ranging from ghost villages and time travel to postal pranks. He is, however, at his happiest performing in the back room of a pub. It is worth noting that David is a medical man by rumour only; approach with extreme caution, particularly if he offers to whip out your tonsils in exchange for a packet of biscuits.

drbramwell.com
@drbramwell

JO KEELING

A devotee to slow and thoughtful journalism, Jo is proud to be part of a growing subculture of independent publishers. She is the founder of *Ernest Journal*, a magazine for the curious and adventurous that encourages readers to slow down and appreciate simple pleasures while rekindling a thirst for knowledge and exploration.

She is also the editor of *Waterfront*, a magazine for Friends of the Canal & River Trust, which satisfies her healthy inclination towards Victorian invention and lets her geek out over river etymology and ox-bow lakes. She also curates talks and immersive experiences on the theme of water and landscape for festivals.

As well as co-authoring *The Odditorium*, Jo contributed to *Wild Guide: Devon, Cornwall and South West* (2013), writes for *Lonely Planet, Countryfile, Sawdays, The Simple Things, The Guardian* and *Independent* and has spoken about independent publishing for a Guardian Masterclass and various other events.

A lido lover and sea swimmer, Jo is never happier than when immersed in water or when rambling over northern moorlands and exploring Britain's peculiar corners.

www.slowjo.co.uk
@SlowJoKeeling

ernest.

Ernest Journal is a magazine for the curious and adventurous.
It is a guide for those who appreciate true craftsmanship, who are
fascinated by curious histories and who care more for timeless style
than trends. Over the past three years, the journal has covered
such diverse subjects as sea monsters, untranslatable words, wild
man mythology, Victorian diableries, Brutalism, Iceland's Huldufólk,
ghost radio stations, post-apocalyptic glass making, the psychology
of Antarctic exploration, cryonics, Futurist cooking, solargraphy,
memory palaces, a lost Nordic language discovered in the North
York Moors and a room filled with 900 frozen brains.
ernestjournal.co.uk

'It's hard to describe the excitement I felt when I first held a
copy of *Ernest Journal*. It was as though someone had reached
into the deepest recesses of my mind and turned its muddled
lumber into an exquisite object. It was like that moment when
you meet someone and know you'll be friends for life. I have
to force myself to read it slowly. Every word, every beautiful
illustration feels charged with meaning and makes me want to
pull on my boots and wander off into the unknown.'
John Mitchinson, *QI*

'*Ernest Journal* is ridiculously beautiful and almost too wonderful
to read. Getting the latest edition is like holding the new album
from your favourite band before you've played it.'
Wolfgang Wild, *Retronaut*

Launch of the Year, Digital Magazine Awards (2014)
Shortlisted for Magpile's Best New Magazine (2014)

②DDITORIUM

The *Odditorium* podcast, which features episodes on people covered in *The Odditorium: The tricksters, eccentrics, deviants and inventors whose obsessions changed the world* (Hodder & Stoughton, 2016) is a portal into the fringes of culture: its mavericks and pranksters, adventurers and occultists, artists, comics, eroticists and even the odd chef. Each episode features a guest speaker recorded before a live audience. It is ably hosted by author David Bramwell and comic actor Dave Mounfield (BBC Radio 4's *Count Arthur Strong's Radio Show*) who frame the topic with their mixture of humour, insight, silliness and an obsession with biscuits. The show is produced by Andrew Mailing and double Sony Award-winner Lance Dann, whose sound design adds an extra layer of wit and spice to the mix. The podcast broke into iTunes' top ten Arts and Culture list, has featured in *The Guardian*'s 'Top 50 Essential Podcasts' and continues to tour with live events at festivals.

Why does a dolphin's vagina corkscrew? What is the best song to commit suicide to? Why is a hanged man's severed hand so valuable? What is the origin of the rudest word in English? Why are we so obsessed with big willies? Subscribe to the podcast and you will find out all the answers you need, and a few you don't.

Subscribe to the *Odditorium* podcast on iTunes, Stitcher or your favourite podcatcher, oddpodcast.com

'A taste for genius matched by eccentricity'
Bella Todd, *The Guardian*

contributors

We're honoured to have worked alongside this talented team of authors, artists and mystery seekers.

MATT IREDALE

Matt is a copywriter, writer and editorial assistant for *Ernest Journal*. Consumed by a love of science, his writings touch on socio-economics, the avant-garde and the intricacies of translation. Previously a cinematographer, he founded Eyes On The Screen, a website devoted to obscure and forgotten cinema from around the world. **mattiredale.com**

JOHN HIGGS

John is the author of *Watling Street*, *Stranger Than We Can Imagine: Making Sense of the Twentieth Century*, *The KLF: Chaos, Magic and the Band who Burned a Million Pounds* and *I Have America Surrounded: The Life of Timothy Leary*. He lives in Brighton with his partner and two children, and a lion. **jmrhiggs.blogspot.co.uk**

BRENDAN C. BYRNE

Brendan's fiction has appeared on *Motherboard*, *Flapperhouse* and *Flurb*, his non-fiction in a variety of querulous organs. He lives in Queens, New York. **@BrendanCByrne**

LEILA JOHNSTON

Leila is a writer and artist working with speculative science, digital and humour. Her work has been shown at The Lowry, The British Science Festival and the Brighton Digital Festival. In addition to journalism and digital arts commentary, Leila has authored several books, including fantasy gamebook *Enemy of Chaos*. **finalbullet.com**

JEN ROWE

Jen writes short fiction with a speculative edge; she has had poetry and plays performed on stage and was published in the *Henshaw Two* anthology in 2017. As well as writing, Jen is an actor, workshop facilitator and an improviser with The Maydays, for which she writes blogs about performing. **jennyrowe.co.uk**

MARK PILKINGTON

Mark Pilkington is the author of *Mirage Men*, the book and documentary film, and has contributed to numerous anthologies and publications. He is the founder and director of Strange Attractor Press and edits its occasional journals. When not squinting at words, Mark plays synthesizers in musical projects including Teleplasmiste, Urthona, Rainbow Unit and The Begotten. **strangeattractor.co.uk**

IAN 'CAT' VINCENT

Ian 'Cat' Vincent is a *Fortean* journalist and occultist: he is a leading member of the British Discordian revival. His articles and spoken word performances focus on the relationship between myth, fiction and magic. His first book *New Gods and Monsters*, on the evolution of pop culture beliefs, is forthcoming. **catvincent.com**

acknowledgements

The authors would like to extend thanks to: Daniel Schreiber, Dr. Alastair Goode, James Shaw and the Bodleian Library, The Panacea Society, Kendall Whitehouse, Chris Parkinson, Chuck Tingle, Celeste Appel and the Unarius Academy of Science, Murray Ballard and Alan Moore. With particular thanks to our publishing team at Hodder & Stoughton: Jonathan Shipley, Iain Campbell, Christina Wood and Antonia Maxwell as well as Lance Dann, Andrew Mailing and Dave Mounfield from *Odditorium* podcast. Finally, to our diligent researchers and writers Guy Lochhead and Matthew Iredale and to all of the *Ernest Journal* team for working tirelessly to design and edit *The Mysterium* – thank you!

PHOTO CREDITS

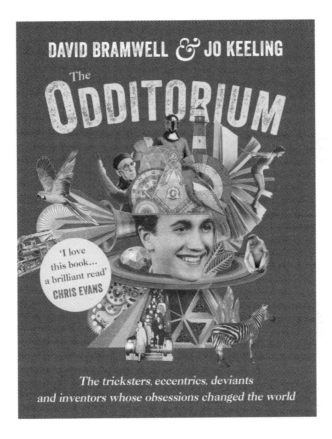